THE CAVE OF APPALACHIA

THE CAVE OF APPALACHIA

Kyle Garvin Curry

NEW DEGREE PRESS

COPYRIGHT © 2021 KYLE GARVIN CURRY

All rights reserved.

THE CAVE OF APPALACHIA

ISBN

978-1-63676-871-7   *Paperback*

978-1-63730-171-5   *Kindle Ebook*

978-1-63676-344-6   *Digital Ebook*

AUTHOR'S NOTE

"Horror is dead," my friend told me over a late night *CSGO* match.

"Oh yeah," an apathetic reaction from my drained 2:00 a.m. brain was all I could manage.

"It's murder this and slasher that. Overdone blood, supernatural and one-dimensional characters."

I sat there for a moment soaking in what they were saying. *Is horror really dead?* Sure, there were tropes that were done to death, but in my mind to call something dead would mean that no one wants to watch it anymore. This happened with the fall of the Western and the two-year 1983 Video Game Crash in the United States. Both were oversaturated, faced some form of an industry restriction, and fell into a pattern of using the same tropes over and over. However, both video games and the Western would eventually return.

So, I kept wondering, *Is horror dead?* It's possibly oversaturated. However, I would say that with modern communication channels and ease of viewing and reading new entries to anything, it's healthily saturated. People mostly cherry-pick what they want. There is little in the way of restrictions, other than what people want to read, so that argument is practically invalid.

"You're wrong," I said about four rounds later.

"What are you talking about, Kyle?" both of my friends were reasonably annoyed at me for poorly performing in these games.

"You're wrong. Horror is not dead."

"We've been off that topic for a while, *insert obscene name calling here*," my one friend said.

"Also, you're wrong," said the one who made the initial comment.

"I'll prove you wrong," I told him.

About a year later, and here we are with a conversation that may or may not be transcribed perfectly. There was one obstacle to overcome: what would this be about?

I thought about that a lot. There are certain things everyone expects to find in certain places. If you watch the news, there will be something bad; if you watch action, there's an obvious hero; if you read the paper, there's going to be opinion articles that go on forever about nothing; and if you read a math textbook, someone is going to be buying too much damn fruit.

"So, what's your point," you read in your own voice.

The point is that the worst horror we can think of is what humanity is capable of. I believe that *Schindler's List* by Stephen Spielberg and *A Night to Remember* by Walter Lord are horror. These are lifted from the pages of history. For the most part, it is what has actually happened. However, not all horror is as intense with fear or shock. No, some horror is long, drawn out, inescapable, but less shocking to those who don't experience it. A horror that is not comfortably or openly talked about by those who experience it.

We all know it exists, happens, and we all know or have met someone who experiences it. In all truthfulness, struggling with mental illness is living your own horror story. I say this for the reason that we seal ourselves off. We seal ourselves off to those who know us and those who don't.

Many times, we don't like to talk about it, because in reality while people will say that it's okay to talk, they will then get pissed if we're not comfortable speaking about it or even if we do talk about it. When we do feel comfortable talking about it, there is the tendency to throw everything out at once. That becomes overwhelming to the listener and causes frustration. It is because people—outside and inside—get frustrated by not understanding what the illness is. We all deal with our illnesses differently, and I will go as far to say that not a single person will handle it the same as another.

And still, we continue to seal ourselves off from those who do fully understand what is happening and are trying to help, because we are fearful of what we've experienced. But, thankfully to a few, we realize that and try to fix it, many times to no success.

CHAPTER 1

THE CONODOGUINET

?

And His light came down and peeked through the canopy of the sugar maples, hemlock pines, mighty oaks, regal birches, and even the timid aspens; it danced around ivy, moss, and vines onto the ground that was damp with that day's morning dew. Little lightning bugs plagued the grass surrounding the boat dock and swarmed up in fury as an old, green pickup truck and red trailer coasted backward down into the launching bay.

The old, flat canoe trailer made a soft splash in the water, sending ripples only a few noticeable meters. Minnows scurried around the small ramp, and a snake slithered out from the underside of the ramp-side rocks, avoiding the incoming waves. The trailer sunk further into the cool, semiclear creek water just enough for two small boats to barely touch the water's surface.

Two kids stepped from the vehicle: Clarkson and Kord, seventeen and sixteen, respectively. Clarkson had pale, white, freckled skin. He tended to lean to one side or slouch forward, at least when he wasn't in trouble—which if he was, his back shot up like a rod. He was short, standing at four feet, eleven inches, and he wore his thick, black hair combed into a "flop" style like a 1950s greaser. Light blue eyes with faint bags underneath, round-pointed ears that went straight back and could be individually moved, plus the absence of facial, arm, and leg hair would define his police description.

Kord, on the other hand and knowing him better, looked to be the complete opposite. He stood five feet, six inches, and his back was almost always straight. His skin was tanned to the degree of a farmer's, though he wasn't, and had hairy legs with only peach fuzz on his arms, no facial hair—like his best friend—and short, stubby, blond hair capped off his head.

The two boys had unlatched the kayak and canoe from the trailer and pushed them out into the water, holding on to the tethers as if the vessels were dogs trying to break their leashes. Kord's kayak boasted a sharp yellow color—though he'd nicknamed it "The Orange Bolt"—and was about the average weight, sixty pounds, a little heavier than his cattle dog. The canoe was old, a leftover from their now dissolved scout troop, auctioned off by the withering sponsor. Clarkson and Theresa named it "The Great Western Duck." It was a dull buff hue, with a fading scout's council symbol and troop number at the front, and it was made out of polyethylene. Heavier than the kayak, but not by much.

Theresa, Clarkson's older sister of twenty, parked the truck and trailer in an open spot and carried their packs down the launch bay.

Theresa was the more outgoing of the two siblings present, despite previous run-ins. She stood taller than both boys at five feet, eleven inches. Her black, shoulder-length hair was as thick as her brother's. She had deep blue, round like golf balls eyes that stood out from her brother's, and high cheek bones inherited from her late father. People called her a beautiful child and probably still would if she socialized more.

Clarkson had tied a knot around the canoe's yoke and ran the rope a few times through loops in the gear and wrapped it around thwarts on both sides of the yoke before tying off the finishing knot. Theresa stepped into the back of the canoe, followed by her brother in the front. Clipping the GPS to his belt, Clarkson helped his sister push themselves out into the creek. Kord followed shortly behind them; his kayak wobbled before balancing out in the open water. Kord took in a deep, tired breath, and exhaled. He looked to Theresa and Clarkson, and then they paddled out into the cool waters.

When the noon heat came, they let the current of the Conodoguinet take them downstream. Just like any other August day in their neck of the woods, the morning had fooled them into the course of the day. It was hot, and even after paddling themselves under the shade of the trees, it was agony for the three—even the leaf bottoms were dry from the heat. It did not help that they could only float so long underneath the canopies until either the canopies ended, or some driftwood and branches forced them away from the muddy, raised shoreline.

Clarkson held an old, portable Panasonic RX-5010 radio in his lap. He was fiddling with it, trying to find a station that could be tuned into without too much static. He would slowly turn the knob on the right while adjusting the height and angle of the antenna. What was once a warm gray plastic shell had yellowed and dulled to an uneasy spotty brownish-yellow and gray coating that no amount of cleaning or disinfecting could change. The metallic finishing on different parts of the device no longer complemented the rest of it. Nor did it complement Clarkson's vision, because every little shake and sway would bounce the sunlight one way or another into his eyes, blinding him for just little moments at a time. Clarkson flicked the switch for FM to FM-Stereo back to FM, then AM to FM, hoping something would come through.

"Any luck there, Clarkson?" Kord asked as the current tapped his kayak against their canoe.

"Nuttin'," Clarkson said. He flipped the radio over, took out the C batteries and put them back in. "We're not even in a dead area. I thought I fixed this thing."

"Here, lemme see it," Kord said and put his hand out, waiting for the radio.

Clarkson waved Kord's hand away and said, "Oy. Y'all—I got it."

Kord turned himself in his kayak just enough to look at Theresa. She put her hands up and huffed out a laugh. Clarkson was focusing everything he had on the radio. He balled up his right hand into a loose fist and slid his thumb around his fingertips. He wiggled his lower jaw back and forth, chattering his teeth. He bobbed his head, shook it, looked down to his right, and rolled his fingers on the back of the radio, tapping it. He sighed and held the radio out to Kord. Kord grabbed it, chuckling.

"Oh. Shut it," Clarkson said, crossing his arms.

"What? I didn't say anything." Kord fiddled with the knob on the right said of the radio.

"Exactly," Clarkson said.

Kord poked out his head like a chicken and looked out of the corners of his squinted eyes at Clarkson. He raised his forearm up from the radio and rolled up his palm. "I'm sorry, what?"

"Ya laughed at me," Clarkson said with a wiggle in his head.

Theresa picked up her oar and bonked the top of Clarkson's head, "Will ya stuff it, ya little priss?"

Clarkson recoiled his back and yelped as the cold creek water from the oar ran down the back of his shirt. He whipped around and pointed at his sister with an open palm. His mouth dangled open, but nothing came out. Clarkson relaxed his hand, methodically bending each finger individually. His lips curled back into his mouth while he patted the top of a plastic bucket that held his sleeping bag, keeping it dry. He turned back around, keeping his eye on his sister.

Kord was holding the tip of the radio antenna in his right hand. Raising his left hand in a knife-hand, he adjusted the angle of the arm. The signal fluctuated between a noticeable but not understandable voice and loud static. He continued to slowly move his arm.

"Thi…seven point three…Er…" came from the radio.

Kord turned the knob.

Guitar noises and "fsssshhshssh" came from the radio.

"I think it's just something up with the antenna," Kord said. His kayak started drifting away from the canoe.

"Just something with the antenna," Clarkson mocked Kord.

"Yeah, ya know, I don't remember askin' for ya sass," Kord said.

"I don't remember askin' for your opinion," Clarkson said.

"You did when you handed me the radio," Kord said, looking snidely at Clarkson.

Clarkson just sat there and shook his head.

"I thought you were supposed to be the one good with radios, dude," Theresa said.

"And I thought you were supposed to be the one good with being responsible," Clarkson said, turning his head around slowly.

"Is that really all ya can think of as a retort?" Theresa said with a smug smile, looking down on her brother.

"Ah, well, ya see here, Clarkson is an absolute pillock when he knows he's on the losing end," Kord said, mimicking an announcer's voice.

"We all knew the truth, ya didn't have to say it," Clarkson said. He rolled his eyes.

"But being Captain Obvious is my only redeeming quality," Kord said, folding the antenna back up.

"You're Captain Something alright. Yo, wait, don't you have your Walkman with ya?" Clarkson asked. He put his hand on Kord's kayak, guiding it back to the canoe.

"Yeah, but it's in my bag," Kord said, patting the top of the radio. "We can try the cassettes when camp's set up. Speaking of…" He handed the radio back to Clarkson.

Clarkson took it and put it behind him. He shifted his weight and leaned a bit so he could unclip the GPS off his belt comfortably. Clarkson pushed the operating buttons on the bottom of the device's face as if it were a Game Boy. He sniffled and shook his head, blinked his eyes rapidly, then sneezed into his elbow. Clarkson raised his head and let out a groan followed by another sneeze.

"Stop it," Theresa, said.

"Shut up," Kord said at the same time.

"Wow, thanks," Clarkson said. "Bastards," he mumbled.

"I'm a woman," Theresa said.

"That makes me one, too," Kord said.

"Ya, keep tellin' yourself that," Clarkson said with a snide grin toward Kord.

"I'm telling Mom," Theresa said.

"Go ahead, and I'll just accidentally forget to water the flowers," Clarkson slurred, digging himself a deeper hole.

"Dude, you didn't have to go that far. Maybe I will tell her now," Theresa said.

Clarkson turned around and looked her dead in the eyes, "Bitch, you won't."

"How much further?" Kord asked before Theresa could say anything.

"Well, another mile to the campsite. It's actually that little opening right down there where the trees are open and there's mud. If you can see it that is," Clarkson said. "Then it's another two miles to the cave. Sun sets at eight tonight and it's noon right now," Clarkson finished, clipping the GPS back onto his belt.

"I don't feel like rowing in this heat, so let's just coast. The water's faster up ahead anyways, so we'll paddle with that. In the meantime…" Kord leaned back in the kayak seat, sighing. He dangled his hand over the edge of the kayak and let his fingertips glide along the water's surface. He rested his head on his shoulder as he wiggled his finger and watched the soft ripples break on his kayak and the canoe.

"Watch your fingers, Kord. Remember when that moccasin or whatever got ya?" Clarkson asked.

"Oh, it wasn't a cottonmouth. First off, it felt nothing like a cottonmouth. Secondly, cottonmouths aren't in PA. Our water snakes just look like them. You got that wildlife badge with me," Kord said with slight agitation.

"Look, I didn't remember its name, and I also didn't pay attention, ya know damn well. But either way, was it a good experience?" Clarkson looked at Kord.

Kord stopped and thought and pulled his hand out of the water and back onto his kayak paddle. Kord patted his kayak oar handle, and Theresa coughed into her elbow.

"Well, in the meantime…wanna play tip-a-canoe?" he asked and flashed Clarkson and Theresa a smug grin.

Clarkson let go of Kord's kayak and pushed him away. Kord's grin got even wider.

As they approached their destination, Clarkson and Theresa eyed up the ramp and launched their canoe toward the shore, hoping to glide up it. The loose mud at the base of the ramp kicked up and made the water murky. A rock hidden within the mud shook both the canoe and its occupants.

Clarkson clenched his teeth and recoiled at the sudden jolt. He jumped out of the canoe, splashing water up his legs onto his swim trunks while mud seeped into and buried his water shoes. As the mud settled and dispersed in the water, Clarkson bent over to check the canoe. Other than a scratch to the paint, no damage had been done to the canoe itself. Clarkson let out a long, relieved sigh and picked up the offending rock.

A crayfish briskly vacated its hiding spot, startling Clarkson. The thick mud around his feet held him still, throwing him off balance and onto his butt. The cold water burst up and cascaded over his shoulders. All the while, Kord, meandering not too far from the ramp, was watching a trout. It had caught some of the minnows, and then it caught the crayfish.

Clarkson, defeated, sat there for a moment in the mud. He stood up and wiped the mud off himself using the water of the creek. Bending over, he dug his feet out from the enveloping wet earth. Clarkson's feet squeaked and sloshed with water draining out of them at each step up the muddy shore. The further up he trudged, the firmer the ground became. Theresa tossed him one end of a rope—the other end tied around a ring on the front of the canoe—and Clarkson tied it off to a thick tree.

Theresa slid herself out of the canoe, expecting to touch creek bed with little effort. Her eyes bulged as water quickly rose up to her chin and splashed over her head. Holding on to the side of the canoe, she made her way toward the shore, the sludge and little creek bed critters attempted to sabotage each step. She waddled and trampled her way ashore as gracefully as her brother had and walked over to him. Her wet, black hair was matted and covered her face.

Clarkson bit his tongue and wiped his sister's hair back behind her ears, revealing her unamused ten-thousand-yard glare. Tips of her hair drug across her cheek like a bug against a windshield.

Theresa closed her eyes, breathed in deeply, and shook her head like a dog, flicking water droplets against her brother that stung like bee stings.

Clarkson put his arm up in defense and looked out toward Kord still in the creek.

Kord, for the most part, was still watching a trout that swam circles under the kayak. Kord paddled forward, and the trout followed. He paddled backward, and the trout followed. He dangled his finger in the water, teasing the trout, and the trout lunged to bite it. Kord got startled and rolled his kayak, scaring away the trout. Kord's head broke up through the water. He gasped for air, grabbing onto the kayak. From the shore, Theresa and Clarkson laughed to Kord's annoyance.

"There's your tip-a-canoe," Theresa shouted back with full glee.

"Doesn't count. I didn't do it on purpose," Kord shouted back.

"Screw me, it doesn't count!" Theresa shouted, bewildered.

"I'm not that easy, I got a price," Kord retorted.

"Oh you are just sick," Clarkson said, holding back a laugh.

"That's supposed to be my line," Theresa said.

"Yeah, but I'm your real brother and he's the unofficial brother. The faux brother. The one we got from the lost and found. And some other synonyms I can't think of," Clarkson said.

"Fine, fine. Oh hey," Theresa grabbed Clarkson's arm. "By the way, you read your letter yet?" Theresa asked.

"Don't, I'd rather not right now," Clarkson said, walking back down to the canoe.

Meanwhile, Kord felt for the cockpit, and once he found it, he ducked under the water, reemerging in the air pocket of the cockpit. Holding on to the sides of it, he sunk himself below water and shot himself back up, flipping the kayak back over. Kord then swam toward the shore, pulling the kayak with him—his paddle drug underneath the water connected to his wrist by a strap.

"Clarkson. Hug me. I'm wet," Kord said with open arms.

"Oh please, I'm too young still," Clarkson said, grabbing the grip of a trunk from the canoe.

"Being young is when you try to get the awkward experiences out of the way," Kord said, grabbing the other side.

"In that case, am I sleeping in your tent tonight?" Clarkson asked. They walked the trunk up the ramp.

"Maybe. Anything special planned?" Kord asked.

"Ya betcha. It's called sleep," Clarkson said.

"Never heard of it. Is it safe?" Kord asked. They placed the trunk down at the top of the ramp.

"Well, doctors recommend about seven hours a night for us younger folk," Clarkson said.

"Well then we must try it if that's the case," Kord said. He turned and with a straight face at Theresa said, "Oh yeah, we're all wet."

Theresa pushed him into the water.

The small camping site they were at did not have a parking lot, nor was it very accessible by road; the only way to get to it was by the creek or by a skinny trail. What the site lacked in accessibility was made up for by space. It was one of the few camping sites not accessible by road to have a maintained bathhouse. Included within the campsite were wooden tent platforms, a picnic table, and a predesignated fire ring made of cast iron.

The three finished up loading the boats and pulled them out of the water on the mud, tying them off to a tree for good measure. It wasn't long for them to set up camp—eleven years of camping in the scouts will do that to a person. The Dutch oven was ready to go over some coals. The tents were pitched, Kord in one, Theresa, unable to sleep or feel safe alone in a tent, with Clarkson in the other. A piece of paracord was hung up as a clothesline, and on it hung the three's trunks and other wet items.

Kord rested in a fold-out chair with no backrest and scissor legs. Down each side of the chair, his full name had been written in a black permanent marker. Over the years, since he inherited the chair from an older scout, the marker had been bleached by the sun and scuffed by natural erosion. It had gone from a chair that was still like new to a chair with a sagging seat that had already been replaced multiple times.

He reached for his waterproof backpack to look for a cassette tape. He unzipped the first front pocket, and he nudged the Walkman to the side, grabbing the first tape his fingers hit.

"Yo, Clarkson?" Kord shouted over to Clarkson, who was tinkering with his radio.

"Wha?" Clarkson looked up from the radio.

"Ya like jazz?" Kord asked.

"Not really," Clarkson said and shrugged.

"Okay good, 'cause this is Meatloaf," Kord said, tossing the tape to Clarkson.

Clarkson caught it and took the tape out of the jewel case. He slid the tape into the unit, pressed play, and without any flaw, it started playing right where the tape was last stopped. Clarkson hung his head and admitted defeat. He stopped the tape, put it back in the case and tossed it back to Kord.

"Well, if it can play, it can record," Clarkson said.

"Why's that important?" Kord asked.

"It's not. Just means the whole cassette function works… hopefully," Clarkson said, putting the radio down.

"Alright, who's cooking dinner?" Theresa asked, stepping out of the bathhouse.

"Nose g—" Kord started, realizing both Theresa and Clarkson were ahead of him, "I guess I am."

Kord pulled out a small notebook, recipes scratched inside. Following it, he made a type of soup that resembled chicken pot pie. To the annoyance of the siblings, and my own, he said it was done "Lancaster style."

CHAPTER 2

FIRE AND DEPART

?

A dying fire flickered and danced about in its cage with the energy it had left. Charcoal built up underneath it, giving the yellow and reddish flames an orange back glow. Theresa was resting in blissful safety, breathing to the slow, calm, monstrous pulse of the nightly wind. The bugs of the island chirped and sounded off as the crashing creek waves promised a solitude away from their immediate predators. Clarkson and Kord sat still awake around a fire whose crackles gave conversation to them, translating the creek's voice.

Kord rested in his fold-out chair. To alleviate the pressure of his body weight, he leaned forward on a stick with a charred tip stuck into the rocky gravel area where the fire pit sat.

Kord agitated the fire, poking it. The fire whipped about and cried its sparks into the dark air in protest to the disturbance. The unrhythmic popping and crackles of the fire knocked Clarkson from the spell the fire casted upon its sleeping prey. He shook his head and fluttered the encroaching smoke from his eyes. Clarkson looked to his right to see his sister fast asleep in her chair. He stuck out his leg and nudged his sister's foot.

"Yo, sis," Clarkson said. When she did not answer, he nudged again harder. "Sis."

"Eh," she said, still just as asleep.

"You're asleep. Go to the tent," Clarkson said just before yawning himself.

Without skipping a beat, she slid her feet off a stump she used as a footstool, stood up from her chair, and shuffled her feet across the ground to her tent. Gravel sifted and dust kicked up into the air while Clarkson looked on to make sure she did not fall. Theresa pulled open her tent flap, the zipper shrieking in the quiet night. She took her only two steps, and the flap closed up. Then a loud thump echoed from her tent, and Clarkson looked back to the fire. He leaned back in his chair and rested his cheek into his palm.

"She had her sleeping bag and ground mat rolled out before she flopped down, right?" Kord asked.

"Oh, probably. She's fine," Clarkson said with a sigh.

The last fuel to the fire's life split and collapsed to the ground. The coals glowed and shined brightly enough for Kord and Clarkson to see each other, but it did not boast the strength it once had. Kord finished messing with it and shifted his weight back onto his chair. The wood squeaked and groaned like an elder with a soured back, and with that, he went back to leaning on his stick.

Clarkson got up and walked to his tent, taking care to step over his sister. He unclipped his small trunk and reached in. Clothes rustled, his mess kit clinked, and plastic clicked off plastic. He walked back out to the fire carrying a small guitar case. It was only about the length of Clarkson's whole arm, about the perfect size for a child. He sat back into his chair and laid the case over his lap. Kord watched him with tired and curious eyes.

Clarkson sighed. His fingers were in position to unclip the latches, but he only ran his fingers over it. He breathed in, flicked the latches up, and breathed out. The top opened slowly, and Clarkson grabbed the bridge of the guitar and pulled it out with gentle care. Under the body of the guitar was an unopened enveloped signed "from Dad" in blue ink. Clarkson looked at it briefly and shut the case.

"You ever going to read that, Clarkson?" Kord asked.

"Someday, when I'm ready," Clarkson told him.

"Has Theresa already read the one she got?" Kord asked.

"I don't know. I would assume so. She handles these things better than I do," Clarkson said.

"She handles most things better than you. If I'm to be frank," Kord said and grinned.

"Ha ha. Ha ha. Mr. Funny Man over here," Clarkson said, rolling his eyes.

Clarkson strummed each string and adjusted their pegs as needed. He played a few practice chords then hesitated on a few more. He scrunched up his face and whickered. His eyes grew puffy and red, but they did not water.

"I guess I should count myself lucky, well, both Theresa and I lucky," Clarkson said.

"Hmm? Why's that, Clarky?" Kord asked, his eyelids getting heavy.

"Well, I mean, I knew both my parents, and they truly loved each other, and that love was also given to us. They were both always there for us. They weren't ever divorced at all, and we were never in your boat," Clarkson stopped and winced at what he spoke.

Little did he know.

"What about Abagail, the oldest of you three caballeros?" Kord asked.

"Well, uh, that is, um, m-metaphorically, that is…" Clarkson said, ignoring Kord completely.

"Heh, and physically. I always just preferred that kayak. I got it from my grandfather. I told y'all that before. Didn't I?" Kord said, helping Clarkson relax.

"Oh no, I don't think ya ever did," Clarkson answered, "You also never told us where he got it, and that whole story too. Not never," he continued, waving his hands and grinning.

"Well in that case, Mr.," Kord looked around, pursing in his lips," Mr., uh, Mr. Asshole—"

"Oh, very creative, Kord. Where'd ya come up with that one?" Clarkson said, clapping his hands.

"Ah, come off it, mate. Wanna hear the story, if ya really never had?" Kord asked.

"Do I have a choice?" Clarkson asked.

"Yes, you do," Kord said and leaned forward with his forearm on his knee.

"Then, naw," Clarkson said.

Kord stared at Clarkson and slowly nodded. He flipped his palms up and shrugged looking one way and then repeated it looking another way. Kord stopped when his weight was shifted fully onto his chair. He looked into the dying coals; they hinted at a red tint, but barely had a glow. He smiled politely at the coal, like a customer service worker who is getting yelled at over something they don't control.

Kord turned this smile upon Clarkson. Though he won, Clarkson still squirmed in his chair with Kord's penetrating eyes and taunting smile. Clarkson squinted his eyes back and wiggled out his hands before placing them at the ready on the guitar. Kord grabbed the fire's water bucket.

Neither moved. It was a standoff of sorts, as if the last two braincells left in existence were being used collectively between them.

Clarkson started to play a few chords.

Kord tipped the bucket, no water yet coming out.

Clarkson frantically strummed some more.

Kord turned the bucket upside down over the coals, squashing out whatever life was left in them.

* * *

Lying in his tent, Kord listened to sounds of the night call to him. The fire was dead, but the wind was not. Its hallowed howling kept Kord staring into the night. He tossed to one side, and his old rectangular sleeping bag crinkled. He tossed to the other, and his ground mat strained, and the ends curled in then flattened back out. He tossed again to his back and blew air through his lips, giving a short buzzing sound.

Kord sat up, bringing his knees up to his chest and rested his head on them. The wind blew strong against the tent's sides, but it didn't bother him much, for his tent was anchored firmly down. He had no worry for the siblings' tent either since their weight alone would've been enough to anchor it, let alone Clarkson's trunk and their anchoring method of "tie everything." Kord sat there and reached for his bag.

Lowering his legs just enough, he propped his bag up so he could reach into it and take out his Walkman. He plugged in headphones and looked at his cassettes, deciding on Vera Lynn's "We'll Meet Again." He slid the cassette into the tray and closed it. Hit play. And sighed, putting his bag aside and bringing his legs back up to his chest, now hugging them.

Holding the jewel case still, he slid the crinkled cover art from it. On the back was a short blurb written by his late mother:

Dear Kord,

Happy Birthday, deary. This is the album of the song you love to hear so much on the radio, and now you can enjoy it the way I did as a kid your age. I'll pick you up from your friends later after work today.

Love, Mom

Almost right after reading it again for the many times he had, the wind calmed. He unzipped the tent flap and poked his head out. The night sky was clear, except for the occasional bat. The moon's light lit up the area with an intensity that Kord had not yet experienced. And since he wasn't going to get much more sleep, he thought it best to take a short walk in the moonlight.

He slipped on his boots, grabbed his flashlight, stepped from the tent, and zipped it up. It was unusually chilly for an August night in the area. Instead of being hot and muggy, it was warm and comfortable. The wind added another soft breeze, leftovers of the rough winds just minutes ago. Still listening to the cassette, he stepped off from the tent, heading more inland from the site, following a small trail.

The dirt trail was canopied by the treetops leaning overhead. Leaves crunched and twigs snapped as he continued through the woods. Watching from a distance, he tilted his head, peering above him through the gaps in the canopy that let the littlest of moonlight in, and took one off the ear cups. Off from the trail, some leaves rustled. His feet snapped into a starting position to run back to camp, as his upper body swept the light around the area.

The flashlight cast an array of light over the shrubs and wooded floor like a lighthouse over its rocks and ocean. Up until he settled the light upon a grazing deer, whose head lifted slowly to meet his stare. It was a white doe, as it bore no antlers, and its eyes were dark as coal—not pitch black, but still quite dark—and in the center of each eye was a single, little, white dot.

A deafening thud echoed from the distance, blaring through his headphones, and the sound of tearing flesh came from the creature, but it did not fall. Instead, the doe turned not just its head but its whole body. Its hooves did not touch the ground. They drug and swung unevenly, and Kord caught a glimpse of another set of appendages, emerging from the stomach, moving the creature. It turned methodically, ignoring Kord, seemingly more upset or intrigued by what had hit it. Moving slowly, gurgling, then breaking off into a sprint, it disappeared.

He followed it with its flashlight. The loud thudding came again, then again, and finally it stopped. Not daring to move his body, he simply darted his eyes around him and slowly swept his flashlight to right, then his left, then his right, and back to his left. He only made it halfway on the last sweep as before him, on the trail, stood the mouth of a cave. Its stalactites jutted down from the entrance like piranha's teeth. Standing on its hind legs, just below the cave's centered tooth, was the creature, stepping closer and closer toward Kord.

Kord took a step back in tandem with it. The steps got faster and faster, until the creature was in full charge. He tried to scream but couldn't. It plunged forward, pouncing onto its prey. As it fell down upon him, time slowed. He looked into the eyes of the beast, and it stared back, morphing into the silhouette of a face he had seen before, back when he was a little kid. Then all at once, time sped up again, and the creature landed on him.

Kord snapped awake in his tent, headphones on, wind calm, light shining through the sides of the nylon and polyester tent. He laid there, only shooting his eyes to the tent door as a shadow of a humanoid creature with several appendages grew larger and larger. It tugged on the zipper from the top of the door flap, and poked its head in.

"Breakfast, sleeping beauty," Theresa said, her hair a mess.

"Alrighty," Kord said within a short, quick breath.

"Here ya go," Theresa said and tossed him a pancake.

It landed right on his face with a distinct plap. And Theresa laughed, making her way from the tent. Kord grabbed the pancake and took a bite out of it.

* * *

They finished breakfast, cleaned up, packed up what little there was to pack up, loaded up, and did whatever else they needed to that could possibly end with "up." Disembarking from the campsite, down to the cave, the clear sky above slowly became overcast with clouds moving in from behind the mountains.

The offshoot of the creek they took grew shallow, barely deep enough for their boats and as mucky as half-melted ice cream. Little did it matter to them at the moment, as they approached the cave. Though the creek was shallow, the land sides, where the shore should be, were growing taller. The bottoms of both the canoe and kayak scudded against the rocks and stones that made up the outshoot of the shore where the cave entrance sat.

Kord stepped out from his kayak and pulled it further on shore, tying it down to a tree, an aspen, that was growing from between the stones that were covered in moss and lichens. From the area around them, this was the only patch of ground that was just rocks, and from the rocks, this tree was the only vegetation other than the scattered, simple vegetation. He grabbed his pack, which was everything he had for their little outing packed tightly together.

He turned to the siblings, Clarkson and Theresa, who had done the same as Kord, and, flashlights in hand, boots on feet, they walked into the cave.

CHAPTER 3

GOING IN

KORD

The cave opening was an odd little outlet. It went back for what seemed a good bit, but it really stopped just after a few yards (or meters for our metric friends), the entrance still fully visible, the light still shining through. Just a few feet in, the main floor of the cave was a small pond of sorts. It was murky, muddy, and a few frogs croaked as we trudged on. I moved to one far end of the cave.

"Hey uh, Clarky," I said.

"Yea, Kordy?" Clarkson replied.

"Was it supposed to be this muddy?"

"Uh, well, never really checked. Just looked it up online and found this cave nearby."

"Ah, so you did the research for the location, but not the terrain of the location?"

"I can do the research now by coming over there and pushing you into the mud, then you can tell us how deep it is."

"He's got a point you know," Theresa chimed in.

"Who does?" I asked.

"Me of course," Clarkson said, as his voice cracked.

"Awe, someone's finally hitting puberty," I mocked at Clarkson.

I scanned my flashlight up the cave wall to the ceiling, seeing a small symbol carved into it that looked like the Star of David. Clarkson and Theresa kept on their back and forth for a minute. I tried to make sense of why there was carving of what look like the Jewish star on the ceiling. If it weren't for the muddy floor halfway up my shins, attempting to steal my muck boots from me, I could almost touch it, just run my fingers over it to see if my mind was playing tricks.

From behind me, the mud made uncomfortably moist slushing sounds. Two pairs of hands grabbed me, my vision spun, and I squeezed my eyes tightly, seeing even more stars.

"Yo, Kord, dude. You alright?" Theresa asked, most of my weight on her.

Theresa drug me to a large dry stone, sitting me down on it. The two siblings had stopped spinning. Clarkson grabbed my cheeks, tilting my head up. I held my eyes open for him, knowing he'd look into my left, then my right, then my left again, pull back, look back into my right and huff. Guess what happened? Just that.

"They look dilated at all, Clarky?" I asked him.

"No. You feel okay?" he asked.

"Yeah, just got dizzy looking straight above me."

"Well, don't do that, and you won't get dizzy."

"No shit, Captain Obvious."

"You okay to keep going, Kord? Sure it was just you looking directly up?" Theresa asked.

"Yeah, yeah. Something just caught my eye," I told her.

"What ya find?" Clarkson, still holding my cheeks asked.

"If you let go of my cheeks, I'll tell ya."

After a brief moment of trying not to laugh, he let go. I got up, both Clarkson and Theresa snapping quick into position to catch me if I fell back again. I gestured to them to stop, waving my hands dismissively for a brief moment.

I waddled my way back through the tracks my feet made through the mud. I stopped just where I stood before I got dizzy, under the star, and put my flashlight in position to point up. After following me and looking up, both Clarkson and Theresa pointed their flashlights to the same point. Theresa, who could reach the low ceiling, even with the mud claiming part of her boots as well, ran her hand over the etching.

Our puzzled looks met and exchanged with each other, and our lights scanned over the rock, mud, and algae growing in the cave as if search lights looking for a bomber. It was for naught since our hand-held search lights landed back upon the star.

"What do y'all make of it?" Theresa asked.

"I haven't a clue," I said.

"If anything, it's just there cause it is," Clarkson said.

"Maybe," Theresa and I said together without attempt.

There was a moment of silence. We were still just looking up into the ceiling at the carving.

"Then the hell we doin'?" Clarkson asked.

"Star gazing," Theresa said.

"Lehayim," I said. "What we looking for?"

I brought my beam down from the ceiling and pointed it at Clarkson's face. He brought his onto mine.

"I found it already, a small passageway over there," Clarkson said, pointing his flashlight, "It's a narrowish crack and we'll have to snake through it. There's a small ledge you'll have to step over, and then it goes down a short ways. Maybe a foot or so."

"Ah, I see. How narrowish?" I asked, keeping my light still on his face.

"Let's find out," Clarkson said, putting his hand over my light to look at me.

Theresa and I followed Clarkson, all three of us flicking mud up in the air when we picked our boots out of the mud. Turned out, it wasn't that narrow, just a bit smaller than a doorway—we all got through with ease. It was dark as hell, though, so we took out my battery lantern.

The lantern took a bit to start up. The batteries I put in the night before had already drained, and it took six AAs in an odd little cradle that slid into battery compartment. The batteries were never easy to replace; it was always a hassle to not bend the metal connectors on the cradle. If it weren't for the fact that this lantern was brighter than all our flashlights combined, we wouldn't bother using it. But that wasn't the case.

As Clarkson had described, there was a small ledge, about the size of a door's stoop, that we had to watch out for. Letting the aurora of the lantern to warm and blanket the area, we discovered out surroundings were really nothing to shake a stick at. The room of the cave we were in was about as large as a small to medium sized room, maybe twelve by fifteen feet and seven feet high. The ceiling dripped water from stalactites. Despite it being the middle of August, it was cold. A shiver came over me, not running down to my spine, but all over. I shook internally, my hands rattled. Goose bumps ran up my arms, my hair on edge. I looked to Theresa, and she looked back at me, an unpleased look on her face, as if she were wearing damp jeans.

It could've been the cold or from seeing that there were three different passageways from this room, and two were illuminated—one in front and on the left. I leaned over to Clarkson.

"Is this an active mine or something?" I whispered.

He shook his head.

"Then why is it lit, Clarkson?" I whispered again.

None of us dared moved our eyes from the passageway. A voice, or voices, came from the same direction, and we killed out lights. All the same, it stayed illuminated, and the voices seemed to intensify. We quietly and quickly ducked into the passageway on the right from where we entered, pinning our backs on the wall.

"Hey, Kord, what are they speaking?" Clarkson whispered.

After pausing for a moment to listen, I said, "I have no idea. There is some English, and also Spanish, and there is some French plus a bit of German."

"Is it that one language that's supposed to be universal. What's it called again? Esperanto?" Theresa asked.

"Yeah, it's called that, but it's too sporadic for that, I think. It sounds more like mumbling," I said.

"Are you able to—" Clarkson started.

A scream coming from down that corridor caught us off guard. We all froze up like criminals in a police's search light. This screaming was soon replaced by laughter, relieving us to an odd degree.

Rocks from the corridor we were in had been kicked up and grabbed our attention. We all had been so fixated on the persons from this other corridor that when I turned my head, I swore to have seen among us a tall, dark figure, half illuminated by the adjacent corridor's light. My soul leaped from my skin, and my eyes widened. The other two snapped their heads to where I was looking, shining their flashlights in the direction. Instead of a person I'd assume to be there, maybe holding a knife or gun, was just a formation from the rock wall that the light gave faux life to. I caught my breath and looked to them.

"Will you two put those out," I whispered sternly at them.

There came the scream again, followed by laughter again.

"Wait a second," Theresa whispered, "that's to a tittle as what came before."

"What does the dot for letters have to do with this?" Clarkson asked.

"Sh," she snapped back to him.

We all listened closely to it.

"Hey, yeah," I started, "they're saying the same thing too."

Theresa held her flashlight like a baton. Clarkson grabbed her shoulder as she started moving. She shrugged him off and probably would've bopped him on the nose if it weren't for her looking first. She continued on, looking down the corridor the sound came from. She turned her head back to us and motioned to follow her. I looked to Clarkson, both of us without amusement on our face. I gestured my head to follow. Clarkson exchanged a head nod with me to follow her, but I retorted with another nod and gestured with my hand. He gave up, shaking his head.

"God dammit," Clarkson said, following behind her.

He drug his feet past me, and I took a step after him. Glancing over my shoulder, the lights had reintroduced the figure to the rocks, with two little white dots on it. I stuck my tongue out at it and followed the siblings. A low-toned humming irritated my ears.

Theresa led our way down this corridor, entering another small room of sorts. The air was much more damp, smelling of mildew and a strong scent like that of wet dogs. The rock was smooth almost all the way around the room. There was a flood light on the floor, shining up against a wall, and lying in the center of the room was small, old cassette recorder. I bent over and pressed stop on it, followed by the ejection button. It did nothing. I tried again, still nothing. I picked it up and held it closer to the lantern, looking inside the deck. The cassette plastic was clear.

"Well, y'all ready to hear something spooky?" I asked them.

"Spookier than this?" Theresa asked, picking up a marionette still in useable shape.

"Yeah, thi—" I started.

"Well damn. Don't think I wanna know then," she said.

"Too bad. This cassette—wait, where did you find that?"

"Next to the fog light," she said with a shrug.

"Uh-huh, well, the cassette still has most of the tape on the starting side," I said, eyeing the marionette with suspicion like it were a spider in the corner of my room.

"How big is the tape?"

"It's only a ninety-minute tape. It's clear, too."

"So not only is it recently played, but it has one of those tapes only prisons can get for whatever reason."

"Yeah."

Clarkson, not saying a word, stood still, in front of the wall that the fog light was shining upon. Theresa and I, having exchanged looks, walked up behind him. We looked at the wall, and upon it was a moon, followed by "Silver is the tongue of the sealed." On the floor was a small trail of water that came from a hole in the wall and deposited through another hole that was in the rock floor. Approaching the wall, I brushed my fingers against the text. It felt dusty, but it didn't rub off.

I held my hand out to Theresa, who handed me the marionette. A string ran from each limb and head of the puppet to a set of two, small, wooden dowel rods. It wore what I assumed was a brown double-breasted suit, due to how it folded over, a light blue tie, and a matching small, flat-cap hat. It had some tuffs of yarn hair that poked out from beneath the hat and round ears that were sewn on with black thread, and two black dots for eyes on a square head. I swore that I could almost recognize it.

I handed the lantern to Theresa, who took it, and I let the strings of the puppet unravel as much as possible. I did the best that I could to make it walk. Instead, the poor thing just gyrated as I drug it forward.

"Yo, buckos," Clarkson called from across the room.

"What?" Theresa asked, turning around with the lantern.

I leaned forward to look around her. Something pricked right into my index finger.

"Gah," I said quietly to myself.

Theresa turned back around to me. I dropped the marionette instinctively to hold my finger and glance over it to see what pricked me. It was a splinter. After pulling it out, I sucked on the wound softly. It didn't bleed.

"I'm good," I said, "What is it, Clarkson?"

"Come check this out," he said.

Theresa and I walked over to Clarkson, leaving the marionette on the ground. Standing behind him, he shined his light down a long, dark tunnel. The light from Clarkson's flashlight just barely reached the end of it. Theresa tried shining the lantern down the tunnel, but it had no effect. None of us dared to walk into the tunnel.

Looking back into the room, I noticed that the fog light gave off a very strong beam that almost filled the whole room. I walked back to grab it, passing the marionette in its gray Nehru jacket with a pinned on blue star. I bent over and picked up the fog light. In the entrance way into this room was again what looked like the silhouette of a person implanted into the wall. I was frozen, the dizziness from earlier coming back to me. I slowly turned the fog light to the direction of the entrance. On the wall, there was a drawing of what looked vaguely like a person. Next to it was what looked like a bird, a bit like a grouse.

I backed slowly away from the wall, eyeing it with suspicion.

"Ya good, Kord?" Clarkson asked.

And with that, the anxiety that had come over me rushed right out. I turned around and nodded at him. Carrying the fog light, I made my way back to the two, and we shined it down the tunnel.

It was indeed very long, but it did have an ending point. We stood there, quiet, still unwilling to go down it. The running of water was the only thing that dared to make a sound. That was, until there was the sound of something moving, a soft roaring sound that also squeaked. We didn't budge. Then it came again. And we collectively stepped back. The sound grew louder as now frantic. We took a few more steps back into the room. A mass of brown and black emerged and came closer to us.

Shrieking little brown puff balls with black appendages erupted out of the tunnel, flapping waxy wings. We had no idea why they were flying this way or what startled them. It wasn't until they were upon us that we pinned ourselves to the sides of the room. Clarkson and Theresa were on the wall with the writing, which was opposite of me. In my surprise of the frenzy of bats approaching, I had dropped the fog light onto the ground, breaking it. Theresa had dropped my lantern on the ground too, but it was still shining brightly.

The bats had finished passing and all at once, there was a loud thudding noise. We took off back for the narrow gap in the wall, Clarkson and Theresa getting a head start, to see rocks falling from above.

"Quick!" Clarkson called, pulling his sister by the hand through it.

Another few rocks had fallen. We got to instant work moving them, Theresa and Clarkson on the outside and me stuck inside, but more only fell upon those as we dug them out. Small holes formed between them, letting some light still through. I hacked up a lung from all the dust filling the room.

"Kord! Can you hear me? Are you alright?" Clarkson yelled from the other side.

"Hack—Y—haaac—yeah. I'm—cough—good," I did my best to say.

I turned on my flashlight, panning over the walls. We were both silent for a minute, and the dust started to settle.

"Any ideas, Kord?" Theresa asked.

"I can't think of anything. Y'all got any?" I asked, sitting down upon a fallen rock.

"Hold up, there has to be something, guys," Clarkson said, sounding frantic.

"Like what?" I asked.

"That one corridor, when we first entered, check to see if there's an opening over there," Clarkson said.

So, I went to go check. It didn't have an immediate end in sight, but it only curved and went deeper into cave. I had checked the adjacent one that we didn't go in. That one came to a dead end. I went back to the entrance that was now plugged up with rocks.

"It doesn't have any end in sight, but it just goes in deeper," I said.

"Okay, well, well, well, there has to be something," Clarkson said, stepping around in a circle in the mud outside, as his tendency to pace when flustered or frustrated.

There was another brief silence. And I guess Theresa was humming to herself? Then she spoke, "Get help."

I could only imagine Clarkson's face.

"I-is that going to be a good idea? Surely there's something we can do," he said.

"No shit, you pillock," I said, "it's called getting help."

"Well, I guess you are Captain Lost this time, ain't ye?" Clarkson asked.

"I ain't lost. I know exactly where I am," I called back.

"Will you two stop wisecracking for a second?" Theresa asked.

"We can. Doesn't mean we will," I answered. The rock was not the most uncomfortable seat I've sat on.

"Fine, fine. Who did you have in mind, hamster?" I asked.

A short pause, then Theresa asked, "Is that me?"

"Yeah," both I and Clarkson answered.

"How am *I* Ham—I am literally taller than both... Never mind. I'm thinking go straight to Smitt," she said.

"Right to the mayor?" I asked.

"Well, you don't have any better ideas. Besides, she keeps her door open and knows us personally," she said.

"That might not be the best idea. I mean, I've had to save y'all's skins from her before," I said.

"Well, let us return the favor," Clarkson said, surprising me.

I sighed. "Okay, alright. I'll be here."

"We'll be right back, Kord," Theresa said.

"And don't do anything stupid," Clarkson added.

I waved my hand, though I know they couldn't've seen it. There was some scraping against rocks, the disturbance of water, and then silence. I took out my Walkman, put the headphones on, put in a cassette, and pressed play.

GOING IN · 43

CHAPTER 4

SMITT'S

CLARKSON

The drive to Ms. Mayor Smitt's residence was long. Neither I nor my sister spoke. We paddled our canoe upstream, fighting against the current, in the hot sun, just to get to a car that was hotter inside than it was out. The canoe was strapped to the trailer, doors were locked, seatbelts fastened, car started, and now we sat outside Smitt's door.

I took a deep breath and looked to my sister. She was clutching and rubbing the steering wheel. I put my hand to her shoulder. She just looked to me and nodded. We stepped out and walked up to the door. Though it was wide open, I drummed my fingers against the door.

"Minuto!" A soft, warm, and firm voice came from inside. "Come in."

I motioned my hand for my sister to go ahead of me and stepped in after her. We waited in the small foyer, crowding the doorway, blocking anyone wishing entering or trying to leave. The stairs were right in front of the door, they were wood with little step rugs applied to them. Next to the steps, in a narrow hallway made narrower, was a skinny bookshelf. On top of which was a small plate and cup decoration stand, both the cup and plate had the Puerto Rican flag painted on the top left, and the Dutch flag on the lower right. Though clean, the wood and golden springs showed their age from when it was made. The walls were mostly bare except for some of Mr. Smitt's calming, beautiful, and humble Leerdam and Dutch landscape paintings that contrasted with Ms. Smitt's colorful, gorgeous, and attention-demanding paintings that I can only describe as being unmistakably Latino.

Is it my fault? I thought. *I should've done more research about it. Sure it's "off-limits," but there's no way that we'd know it was going to cave in. It's not the first place we've gone to that's—*

"Ah, Master and Mistress Sherman!" That soft voice came again.

"Clark," my sister said, elbowing my arm.

I turned my gaze upwards like a puppy who knows he did something wrong to meet Ms. Smitt's gaze change from curious and preppy to a disappointed mother's.

"H-hi, Ms. Smitt," I said under my breath.

"Come on you two. What did y'all break this time?" she asked us, laughing, motioning for us to follow her to the kitchen.

"Well, uh, it's about Kord," I mumbled.

"Say that again, hun?" Ms. Smitt asked, offering up a glass of water to me.

"Um, uh," I muttered after I took the glass and lowered my gaze.

"Something about your broki?" she asked, sitting down.

I fiddled with the glass, taking small, sporadic sips.

"Kord is in trouble," Theresa said, in a succinct tone.

Ms. Smitt's face slowly sank into an unamused expression. The corners of her mouth flattened and contracted closer together. The crow's feet, at the corner of her eyes, flattened out and lost their pertinence. Her head lowered, and her back tensed as she leaned forward. The wooden kitchen chair creaked as she did. The pounding of the ticks and tocks, from what could have been the last analog clock, stretched out time for the next few seconds to feel like the next few months. I made the mistake from curiosity to look her in the eyes. Its distant control isolated the both of us to another realm.

"What type of trouble?" she asked.

* * *

He'll be okay. He'll be okay. He'll be okay. He'll be okay. He'll be okay. I chanted in my head.

Sitting in her office, waiting for Ms. Smitt to come back with some paperwork, I noticed the same small brown stain on the ceiling was now accompanied by a smaller friend. My leg seemed to have a mind of its own, because it would shake even as I tried to hold it still. Theresa just watched me, solemness in her eyes.

"Yo, bro, it's going to be okay," Theresa said.

"Mhmm," was all I could muster.

"We'll get him out."

"Yeah."

Theresa sighed and looked away from me, springing back up when Ms. Smitt walked back in with a notepad and something rolled up under her arm.

"Okay," Ms. Smitt said, exhaling as she did.

Theresa looked to me to speak. I opened my mouth but was unable to let anything out.

"Well, when do we go get him?" Theresa asked for me.

"Right now, there's not much we can do. The absence of rain these past two weeks has left the creek fairly shallow in some spots, and the coming tropics threaten to cause flooding in some of the harder hit areas," Ms. Smitt said, rolling out a political map of the mid-Atlantic states, placing a copy of Truman Capote's *In Cold Blood*, a small brass molded globe, a glass case with a moon rock in it, and a mug that said, "I swear this is just coffee…or tea" on different corners.

"What do you mean? How can it flood if there's been no rain?" Theresa asked.

"Well, Hurricane Danielle is weak, but it's being pushed by Earl," she placed her fingertips on the map at Norfolk, Virginia. "Danielle is assumed to be moving up through the Chesapeake, already dropped to a tropical storm by the time it hit Bermuda, will most likely just become a depression," she wiped her hand up the map along the coast and the inside of Delmarva.

"However," she continued, "Earl is being a prick. Every path we've predicted for it has been made a joke. First it became the southernmost traveling hurricane to turn north. It's hit Georgetown in Guyana and went almost straight northwest over the Caribbean islands and Hispaniola, then Santiago de Cuba to just head for open waters. It was a cat-one when it hit Guyana but was a cat-three by Cuba. It's currently stalled about twenty miles off the coast of Daytona Beach. We have a week, max, before it lands. So, to answer your question, just a lot more rain than the creek can hold."

"So, what does this mean for Kord, Ms. Smitt?" Theresa asked.

"The cave, if the correct one," Ms. Smitt put down another map, this one was topographical, "should have this small outlet after the mouth of the cave. Was it muddy? Feeling like you'd get stuck?"

Theresa and I violently nodded yes.

"Alright, well, you're lucky to be here, because that cave entrance can fill to the ceiling, and that mud is really a pod that's ten feet deep. The dirt is usually washed out and not carried in, oddly. If it were to flood, there are many small corridors that lead to a large underground river that feeds into Yellow Breeches down in Mount Holly. Anyways, if the creek floods, Kord will have to retreat to higher ground in the cave. The only thing we're able to do now is send someone to slide food and water between any possible cracks in the collapse."

"Um, Ms. Smitt, what can we do, Clarkson and I?"

"Head home, clean up, eat, and pray. Take care of yourselves and we'll call you when we need you two. We'll send a couple of officers down to the cave with said necessities for Kord. It's just a matter of keeping him alive."

"T-there's something else, Ms. Smitt," I finally piped up.

"Yes, Clarkson?" Ms. Smitt flipped the short bangs of her shorter hair out of her face.

"There was someone in there before us."

She hesitated. "Did you see them?"

"N-no. There was a light, tape recorder, and marionette in there. Carved on the wall was 'Silver is the tongue of the sealed.'"

She wiggled her head, her eyes wide in confusion. She looked about trying to make sense of what I just said. "I wouldn't think too hard or too much into it, either of you."

"Why?" Theresa asked, "Could there be someone in there with him?"

"Don't think too hard on it."

"*Ms. Smitt*," Theresa said.

"Look, we'll make sure he's fine. I'll file the report immediately and keep you two updated. For now, go get cleaned up and everything. Kord will be fine."

My sister and I got up slowly. Ms. Smitt looked me dead in the eyes, and I looked back.

"I promise. He'll be okay," Ms. Smitt said.

We nodded our heads and left her office without a word. A warm shower sounded nice, but with Kord still in there, it wouldn't do too much to help.

CHAPTER 5

ENTER RAEF

KORD

"Ksssh, Rubber Duck, come in, Rubber Duck. We got ourselves a convoy," I spoke into my Walkman like a CB radio, then lowered it between my legs, hung my head, and sighed deeply. "Come in, Clarkson. Come in on your stupid radio…" It had been four hours, and I hadn't moved around much in this cave.

The rock I sat on was unfortunately slightly wet, about maybe twenty feet from the collapse. I had my little lantern set up in front of me. The only thing I had in the way of entertainment was my Walkman. One can listen to only so much music while sitting on rocks lumpier than my bed before getting restless.

I had attempted to search for that marionette from before, but to no luck. I assumed it got kicked down the hole in the floor or trampled and torn up when those brown oversized marshmallow things came through and we scattered to get out.

I rummaged in my sack for anything to distract me and came across a few books I had packed. The one on top was the Bible. I've never read it but holding it has always provided a sense of security. I was brought up in faith but had never taken the time to read the holy book. Keeping it around was more of keeping—or more truthfully, suppressing—a memory.

    A rock bounced in the distance. I stared down the corridors to the sides of me. I don't know for how long, but I looked back to the Bible and kissed it. Perhaps it was a false sense of security, but it was security, nonetheless.

    "Is that you, Mr. David Lewis? Sir Robin Hood of Pennsylvania, I beckon thy presence to be known, because you're in the wrong cave, sir. A few more miles down the stream, unless I'm mistaken," I said to the darkness, zipping up my pack.

    I waited for an answer, and there was no reply.

    Again, came the sound of a rock. Louder, and it seemed closer. I swallowed a mouthful of cotton and attempted to ignore it. I looked down at my pack and started putting it on, grabbing my lantern.

    "I see, I see. I must be rich, then! If that were truly the case, then I would buy tram and lay rails throughout the city and provide transportation at a small reasonable fee. Oh, three Mexican pesos per chain? Maybe four. Maybe try to get a Roth IRA out of it…whatever that is."

    I lifted the lantern and froze. Across the ground in front of me was a long shadow. I followed the lantern down the shape of the shadow toward the rocks. There was nobody there. But there was a face, a white, pale face with blank eyes, as if it were blind. Unattached to it, but still under the influence of it, were two small wings and a thick, silver ring—that showed a reflection of everything around it as if it were lit perfectly in the cave—right where a neck would be.

    Hello, Kord. Do not be afraid of me, it read to me as a large, dark, skeletonized hand reached for me.

    "Nope!" I blurted out.

Without thought, I took off down the nearest corridor, booking it. I ran. And I ran. Ducked under rocks, rounded bends, took turns in a number of forks along the way. I didn't keep track. All I know is I eventually ran out of breath. I grabbed my canteen, twisted the top of it, and took a long and full gulp.

"Okay, Kord. Okay," I said and patted my hands in the air. "Oh boy. What was that? What was *that*? A white face, skeleton hand, little fuckin' feather wings. What in the hell?"

I felt for a wall and slid down it, sitting.

"Skeletor, I guess? Myah," I said and waved my hands and took another sip. "Gyah-ugh," I bellowed after the sip. "Okay, okay. I…I saw something of my imagination. That's all. Hearing things, seeing things…I'm anxious, that's what. Just some anxiety—being couped up in the dark, that's all. Phew, okay, okay." I popped my lips in a quick rhythm. "Gotta keep my mind occupied. Occupied. Occupied…I gotta pee. Why did I sit?"

Both my knees popped when I stood. I let out a low-bellowed chuckle and groaned as I stretched my legs. I lifted my lantern in front of me and found a faint glimmer followed by a trickle. I waddled my stiff and knee-popping self over to the glimmer. A small pond, about the size of a plastic kiddie pool you could buy off a store shelf. I crouched, holding the lantern close to it.

Muddy, but I could see to the bottom, where water swirled into a little hole. I slowly swept the lantern over the pond. When my hand got to the far wall, water fell upon it in a steady flow. I looked up and tilted my head every which way, but I couldn't make anything out. I flicked the switch to the lantern and put it away, taking my flashlight out instead. It was able to give a better beam of light, albeit in one direction.

Rocks moved again in the direction I came from, faint and distant, but still I was spooked. I breathed in. I breathed out.

I turned on my flashlight and pointed at the pond and followed it to the wall. From the wall, I followed the little waterfall. I stood, and it kept going, and going, and going. My flashlight didn't hit the ceiling.

"Well, shit. How tall is this cave?"

Fifty meters, Kord, a voice said. *You ran into the dark without direction.*

The voice came from inside my head.

"Who's there? Show yourself!" I spun and my foot slipped into the ankle-deep pond.

Nothing answered.

"Oh great, now I'm hearing more things. This some bullshit!" I yelled into the darkness. "I'm lost in a cave, scared shitless by my imagination. *And,* it's darker than the lyrics to 'Whiskey in the Jar.'"

I kicked some loose rocks down the corridor. Turning my attention back to the pond, I dipped a finger into it and lifted it toward my nose. I didn't inhale, but let the scent float up my nose. It smelled like creek water.

"I'm either up or down stream. Either way, I'm without a paddle," I said to myself, brushing my fingers on my shirt.

I rolled my head over my shoulders and shook out my arms and legs, especially the wet one.

"The dark can be a beautiful thing, ya know? You just stop what you're doing, and let the soft somber sounds trickle in through your ears. Those sounds are nice when you're not outside camping and in the middle of the night hear a fox's mating call. You ever listen to those things? It's downright terrifying. You'll be lying there listening to crickets and flowing water then, out of nowhere, *skreee!*"

"Skree! Skre. Skr—" the chambers of the cave answered back.

"At least it's not as bad as if you were to hear your own name said aloud by someone, or thing, else."

"Kord?" A small echo came from somewhere in these chambers.

Perhaps just my mind again.

"Yeah, like that," I mumbled to myself.

"Kord? Kord Clverson?"

Now I knew it was an actual voice, a heavily accented one at that. Any other point in time and I'd be terrified to hear my name in the dark, but honestly, I was more pissed off at this point.

"Is that you, God? It's me, not Margaret."

There was a long pause. I had stopped moving, and there was no further reply or footsteps. A standoff with the darkness around me. At some point I had turned my light out, though I don't remember doing it. I waited. I'm not sure for how long, but it was a while before I heard movement again. Crunching rocks and the mushing of dirt.

"Who's there?" I turned my light on again and flailed it around me. "I have an abnormally large flashlight and it hurts. I know from experience."

"Kord Clverson?" the voice chimed up again, sounding closer.

A lanky man turned around the corner, carrying a flashlight shorter than mine.

I looked him up and down as he took a few more steps toward me. The only thing I moved was my flashlight, up and down with my eyes, methodically. He had tanned, olive skin, bushy eyebrows, and a nose that could take up its own time zone. He held up a badge that glinted light back toward me. The only words I could make out were "Department of" but the shape appeared familiar enough. I don't know why, but it let me relax my guard.

"No…maybe."

This guy just stared at me and flicked his head around. I had assumed he was confused.

"Who's asking?"

He instantly stopped, looked me dead in the eye, and said, "My name is Raef. I am part of an ongoing search and rescue operation for a young man by the name of Kord Clverson. Are you him?"

"I'm him. Kord Clverson, that is me. I don't have a badge though," I said to him, lowering my light.

"Mr. Clverson—"

"I'm not an adult."

"Master Clverson."

"Just Kord's fine," I said and shrugged my shoulders.

He stared at me, lowering his head but not his eyes a tad, and said, "Okay. *Kord.* I am Raef, part of a team sent in here to find you. There is an exit back this way if you just follow me. Are you all alright?"

"Yeah, I'm fine. Just wet," I told him.

Raef reached for a walkie on his hip. He wore fairly casual clothing: jeans, black button-up, and a thin, long, white shirt underneath. He lifted the walkie and spoke into it.

I started looking around us, at the cave walls, not paying attention to what he was saying. When he stopped speaking, there was a beep and a click followed by a "ssss." He spoke into it again. Again, just static, but more in a pattern of someone speaking.

"Damn, cave. It's messing with the signal. These walls are so thick you can barely get anything," he said, looking toward the ceiling.

"Well, it *is* a cave, what did you expect?" I asked him.

He only furrowed a brow, then turned around and told me to follow.

I kept my light on his back as we journeyed deeper into this cave. Something about the situation didn't exactly seem right. The cave got colder, the air moister. Raef was quiet.

We got to a narrow passageway in the rocks and Raef stopped. He pulled a piece of folded-up paper from his pocket, held his flashlight with his teeth and unfolded part of it. He then snapped his head up to the wall of the cave. First to his right, then to his left. He turned around and darted his eyes over the walls. Then his gaze rested on me. Unclipping another little gadget from his waist, he squinted trying to read it and tilted his head.

"Kord. Go back a little bit and see if you find a marking on the wall," Raef said and pointed behind me.

The space was narrow enough that I couldn't turn around, so I had to walk backward. I was cautious and held my hands to the wall. I rounded a bend and watched as Raef's light grew dimmer, and then it was gone. I shuffled inch by inch until my fingers fell into a divot in the stone. It had to be a human-made marking, so I gracefully fumbled with my flashlight, got control over it, and shined it on the wall. Sure enough, it was a navigational compass with a line pointing toward a large *M* with a "33–46" marked underneath it.

"Hey Raef!"

"Yeah?"

"I found a marking here!"

"What does it say?"

"Well," I said and scanned my flashlight across it to make sure I didn't miss anything, "it's a compass with a letter *M*."

"Go on," he said, his voice flat.

"And a thirty-three dash forty-six," I finished and put my hand back against the wall.

"Oh shit." He stomped his foot.

"Raef? Raef, what's wrong?" I directed my flashlight back down the chamber.

"You are not going to like it, Kord."

"Did we take a wrong turn?"

"No, we went the right way and everything, but the entrance is gone."

My heart nearly skipped a beat. "What do you mean *gone*?"

"I mean it's gone."

"Cave entrances don't just vanish like that, Raef."

"There's a reason why these caves are considered off-limits. The soil and rock have been weakened over time. There used to be many openings, but most have been sealed off."

"Ah," I said and leaned toward the side of the cave opposite the marking. "So I suppose they can vanish then."

No response.

"Hey Raef, you there?"

Again, he didn't answer.

"Yo, Raef!"

I snapped my flashlight back down the corridor. Black. I don't mean it was dark like a void, but all the walls were black like coal. Reflective, too. I scratched the wall, and little chunks chipped away with dust. I scanned the flashlight carefully over the ceiling and then the floor and sighed.

"I still need to pee."

CHAPTER 6

SIBLINGS ARE WEIRD CREATURES

THERESA

Siblings are weird creatures, especially brothers. I had been sitting there in our house, in the second floor common area, just to the side of the stairs—used to be an old guest room with no access to central air, but after taking down two walls it now does, feels more cozy now, too—for about an hour watching my brother leave and enter his room. He had the second chorus to "Baker Street" playing on repeat for some reason. He also just kept poking his head out, looking up and down the hallway, and then snaking his way down the hall to the closet then back. The whole time, I was in the rocker in this common area, watching him. I don't think he noticed.

Doesn't matter really, I guess. Clark is a weird kid, but I think he'll be fine. Just as long as he doesn't keep letting his temper get to him. I am always surprised that he'll admit to being wrong with Kord, but he won't with me, but after ten years—give or take—I guess I shouldn't be. Hopefully, the letter that Dad left him will help with that—Dad was always able to calm him down when he was younger by just talking with him, something that young Clark didn't wanna do in general.

Dad left a letter for each of us, even our older sister, Abagail. I don't know what hers or Clark's says, all I know is that I have read mine, bro has yet to read his, and I don't want to know what Abagail's said.

Speaking of that little rat, he popped his head out to sniff around as I finished reading my letter again. He turned down the left side of the hall, swept his eyes over the ceiling, and dropped them on the stairs in front of his door, but his head stayed down the left side of the hallway. One. Two. Three. Yep, three double takes to the stairs after whipping his head to the right side of the hallway. I swear, if he had a rat's ears, he'd use them instead. Clark stepped out of his room, leaving his door cracked, and tiptoed down the hallway…opened the closet…grabbed something that I was both interested in and not interested in at the same time.

"Clarkson!" Our mom shouted from downstairs.

"Yeah?" Clark shouted back, tensing up.

"Can you help in here?"

"Can't Theresa do it?"

"I don't know where she went."

"Alright, just a second," Clark said. Rolling his head back, he then mumbled, "Of course she's off somewhere. Could almost think she has a boyfriend."

Wow, okay, I thought.

He drug his feet to the stairs and sloshed his way down them. The cat waddled his way from the bathroom—next to Clark's room—and thumped down the stairs behind him. I waited a moment, holding everything still that I possibly could have, then got up from the chair, trying to not make a sound. It was quickly apparent that this was unnecessary when I heard the commotion that the chunky furball we call a cat—specifically his name is McFunster—was causing downstairs. Nonetheless, that boy had my curiosity, but that looping of "Baker Street" annoyingly had my attention.

I lurched to Clark's door and peeped inside. Nothing out of the ordinary…yet.

"*Meow*," the little chunker down the stairway called up to me.

I snapped my head around and looked that thing dead in the eyes. It just purred at me in response—we will also call him a "purr-monster"—vibrating the whole landing. Out of all the things I could've done, I sidestepped into my brother's room. I was a perfect squeeze between the crack of the door and its frame.

Being just inside the door gave me the general overview of his room. Nothing out of the ordinary…*yet*. Well, I guess that the "Baker Street" loop was out of the ordinary. But I couldn't just turn it off, Clark would surely know that I was in his room, and I also couldn't pinpoint where it was being played from. Kind of an important part.

Thing is, he had a surround-sound speaker set up in his room—a fancy thing he bought secondhand at a farmer's market over in Williams Grove, and which Dad helped set up. Two speakers sat on the windowsill that was both above and stretched the length of his bed. Another two were flanking his TV underneath a skylight window, along with the main control center of the thing plus his computer and a GameCube. The last speaker was on a stand in a nook just next to his bedroom door.

"Come on, move cat," Clark said, his feet flopping against the hardwood steps.

Oh crap, oh crap oh crap, I thought and frantically looked around for a place to hide.

I got down on my hands and knees, crawling and wiggling my way under his bed. There was only a small bit of viewing space between the floor and comforter that hung off the side of his bed. Even though I was probably safe, and he might not have been able to catch me, I got as close to the wall as I could. I'd rather not speak of the things I found under his bed.

Clark came into his room, turned, and I assumed did his ratty routine before closing the door—I could only see so much. He walked over to a closet door next to the skylight window. He opened the door and went inside, and closed it, and locked it. Why he would lock it, when the lock is technically on the outside of an ordinary bedroom doorknob, I wouldn't ever bother asking—likely I'd never get an answer, other than a huff, anyways.

Wasn't for long though. He cursed himself, though it was muffled through the door, and he left his closet. The door flung open and hit his bed frame, shaking and squeaking closed, laughing as he stumbled out into the hallway. It was foolish, but I attempted to take that time to wiggle out from under the bed with the intent to leave his room, but that rat was quick. He was already back with a box in his hands. I was halfway out from under his bed.

"Sis."

"Clark."

We nodded to one another.

"What a…what ya doing under my bed?"

"Uh, checking for bad stuff."

"Did ya find any?"

"Depends on your definition."

"And?"

He set the box down and closed the door.

"Nope…"

"Don't worry, the 'worse stuff,'" he started, using air quotes, "is on the computer."

"Why would you tell me that?" I asked, digging my face into his regularly cleaned carpet.

"Just thought you should know, considering what's under there."

"Clark."

"Just saying, sis."

"Okay, you know what? You owe me for telling me that."

"Why?" he asked with the most confused look I've ever seen. He quickly followed up with asking, "What ya want?"

"What's in the closet?"

He curled in his lips, stuck his hands in his pockets, and rocked on his feet.

"Clarkson?"

He rubbed the back of his neck, "The, uh…the worst stuff."

He refused eye contact. So, I opened the door. I assume that a teenage boy's Friday nights would've comprised of video games, going out, getting lucky—probably with himself—or something with his friends. Not this weird little rodent. This guy went to hang out at the local college doing…something. Now I knew what.

"Clark, is this a radio set up?"

"Yeah."

"Wow, that's actually pretty cool."

"It's a pirate radio setup…of sorts. With CB."

"What's that?"

"An unregistered broadcasting station. It's more than just a pirate radio. It is able to transmit and receive frequencies from longwave to UHF, including the six hundred, seven hundred, and eight hundred megahertz and tap into governmental channels. I am likewise able to broadcast on any channel if I so wished to hijack it, on almost all frequencies if I do it right, and reroute the connections through the college. That large device on the wall is a jammer of sorts, and on the opposite is a tracker. The thing on the floor is a preamplifier, and each one of those long boxes has wires that are subsequently fed into the walls and wrap around something: pipes, rebar, anything conductive other than the outlets. I can cause and take over dead air at any time. And CB is citizens band radio. Talking," he said in a very matter-of-fact way.

I nodded, and shrugged my shoulders saying, "Alrighty. Anything you left out?"

"Whelp, for what I use it for, it's illegal," he said, staring off into space.

I gawked at the dark closet, its only current illumination coming from the little LCD screens on some of the equipment. Nothing about it was sitting well with me. I know he took from Dad—doing some things in the gray area of the law that no one would honestly care—but I never thought Clark would go beyond what Dad would do.

"Cl-Clark, what if you get caught?"

"Well, it's hard to find in the first place. Especially when the broadcast signal is continuously cycling, and with this little doohickey in this box that I have coinvented with a group of... others...I am able to continue broadcasting on one frequency, while any tracker wouldn't be able to locate the source of the broadcast. It essentially throws the source signal around a five-mile radius, and given the whole house is basically an antenna, hell, to an extent the sewer pipes too, it works quite well."

"But, Clark, what if?" I asked him. I rolled my eyes at his last comment, because even I knew—from the little that

I paid attention to Dad about this stuff—that that was *very* farfetched to be the case—the house and all an antenna.

"If…heh, if," he laughed emptily, "don't worry about it. Go ahead and flick that one switch on the box labeled three."

I did so and the rest of the equipment sprung to life. There was a short, low humming, and then it faded. Clarkson walked past me, took a seat, and played with a few dials. He held a headphone of a headset up to his ear and focused in on a single sliding piece on the box. He flicked a switch with the Bluetooth logo on it, and that "Baker Street" loop finally stopped. He hit another button and unplugged his headset, turning a dial. Voices came over a small speaker inside the closet itself.

"This is the frequency that the local po-po use. It can be f—"

Clark immediately stopped as something caught both of our ears.

"Eighteen, thirteen. Naught. Fourteen, nine, twenty. Naught, nil. Eighteen, one, thirteen. Code Appalachia. No units respond. Repeat. No units respond," said a metallic voice, prerecorded, hollow, and it made no sense to us.

Then it repeated.

Clark and I looked to each other, equally unsettled. Clark turned it off.

"So…" I said, leaning back against the wall.

"Eighteen, thirteen, naught—which is zero—fourteen, nine, twenty. Naught, nil, eighteen, one, thirteen. What in the hell does that mean?" Clarkson asked and looked at me.

"I dunno, bro. Don't ask me."

"I'll need to check that out," he said as he wrote it down on a little pad on the table.

"Mind if I ask you a question, Clark?"

"You can, doesn't mean I'll answer."

"You never answered the if."

"That's not a question."

"Okay, fine. What *if* you get caught?"

He just stared at his pad, rubbing his hands.

I waited for a response I knew would never come, so I changed the subject.

"Alright, what about this: Why did you have the second chorus of 'Baker Street' on repeat for so damn long? And how?"

"The how is my phone. I just set up loop markers on the app I use for music. The why is from Dad. I finally opened his letter. That was my step one."

CHAPTER 7

PAREIDOLIA

THERESA

At three in the morning, I was thrust awake, by what I do not know. But I was stiff in my bed, clenching my sheets, eyes wide—something was not right. I was not scared, but I was alert. Every little sound, every little breath of wind, every little movement of the shadows cast from the tree branches outside against the far wall of my room made my eyes dart around in their sockets like a cat watching its prey.

Another morning. Another day without Kord. If he is still alive, I'd bet he's grown tired of just eating the trail mix, granola, peanut butter, or whatever else he always keeps in his packs during camping trips.

That morning was also the beginning of the third day of rain—near nonstop rain. Every now and then, it would lighten up, but most of the time, it was as if Heaven were crying. For what? There would've been many things. But it was relentless. There was no silence, just rain pounding the roof and thunder rolling across the sky like the charge of a cavalry with lightning as lances and swords.

On the far wall of my room, the shadow of the rain running down the window began to take over the branches of the tree—splotching the walls like it was an aquarium. The splotches formed constellations that the stars at night would've.

One of these constellations caught my attention as it morphed and changed with the running water down the window. It started with one massive reflective bordered shadow that split into five smaller but still quite large spots that formed a square with one in the middle—two branches crossed over the middle one like crosshairs.

Water continued washing the window outside, but the image on the wall stayed motionless—even as water ran over them. That was until a gust of howling wind roared against the window, and one of the spots from the outside squares became absorbed by the middle. Another gusting howl hit the window and with it came the crashing of the waterspout that ran just outside my window. The metal spout grinded against the glass, like someone was torching a daddy longlegs or torturing a group of small mice.

The spots on the wall gave way to more constellations forming on the wall—none of which caught my attention again. The grinding of the spout rang against my ears just how Clarkson's radio does when he can't get a signal. I clutched my ears, running from the room.

The sound followed me into the hallway—illuminated from some light source outside the window. I made my way to the hallway closet—just before the open area next to the stairs—my bare feet slapping the hardwood, but just a level quieter than the chunky cat. I opened the door to the closet, my oversized shirt's sleeves floating onto my shoulders as I reached up to the top shelf. I patted my hands around until

I found the tool bag and pulled it out, placing it on the floor. I pulled a hammer from it.

The floorboards creaked down by my room. Keeping my eyes down the hallway, I felt around in the bag until I found a small headlamp. I took it out, stretched the elastic over my head and turned it on—the hammer still in hand. The floorboards creaked again, and I got to my feet, spinning the hammer in my hand. The door to my room closed slowly, making the distinct squeak it has, as if someone were laughing at you.

I slid the bag with my foot back into the closet; it skipped as the fabric was caught on the floorboards. I closed the hallway door and reached around the wall to flip the switch for the overhead ceiling fan and light in the open area. But only the motor to the fan started up.

"For fuck's sake," I mumbled to myself.

I put my back to the wall, snaking around the corner, still looking down toward my room. Once I rounded the corner, I kept my head still as my eyes scanned up at the ceiling fan. It was spinning on its lowest setting. I hit one of the bookshelves and slithered around it as an extension of the wall. Glancing my eyes back with the direction of the light, nothing moved. I moved for the light cord, but once the headlamp's light moved, something rushed down the hall.

It was dark, shadowed, almost moving among the shadows themselves. Seeing this mass move in the corner of my eye, I rushed for the cord, grabbed it, and stupidly looked into the light as it turned on. It was blindingly bright and made me recoil, tripping over the tufts of the area rug, and fell to the ground.

I bounced my head off of the rocker that I usually sit in and fell to my back as the house shook. I held my hand above my eyes, trying to see. A mass of something sat in the hallway. It was too big to be the cat, but also too small to be Clarkson or Mom, but not too small to be human.

My vision cleared and the mass became clearer, it was human, kinda. It had hair pulled back from its face, held back by a hair band over its head. It sat crisscross applesauce and looked at me. It had two dark voids for eyes, each with a white dot in the center. From the eye sockets, the skin seemed to flow like it were water, down the face, back up its cheeks, to the forehead, and back into the eyes. I wasn't scared, but I was alert. Its hands were on its knees, and the bones to its arms showed through the skin like it were broken leather.

A slow burning rage built in me as I tried to put an actual face to it, and each time I did, there was only one I could think of. I moved to my feet and it did the same. I rolled my neck to my left. It mirrored me. Then rolled to the right. It mirrored me again. I went to open my mouth, and it held a finger to where a mouth would've been. I squinted my eyes and stomped on the area rug, and I made no noise. It shook its head as if to say no. I stomped harder and harder, and it shook its head more frantically.

The house shook more and more, a rush of wind, a rush of flapping was the only thing I could hear. I went to swing the hammer through the air, just to test it, but my arm moved slowly, as if I were trying to move in water. I stood straight. It walked toward me, and I toward it. As I approached it, it became smaller and smaller, until I towered over it—its eye level being just below my chest. I looked directly down at it, and it looked directly up at me. We stood there, unmoving, unblinking, staring each other down. The rumbling grew louder and louder.

The window at the end of the hall shattered, letting in a swarm of birds. Mourning doves, 'jays, orioles, crows, robins, and tufted titmice were led by a raven with a white ring around its neck. The birds distributed themselves, making a deafening collection of calls all at the same time. The raven landed and sat between the eyes of the thing I stood over. The raven looked directly at me and blinked three times.

The thing's hands morphed from its face and grabbed the raven's neck. The raven opened its mouth and made the call of a vulture. The crows descended upon the raven, attacking it, and tore away at it, piece by piece—carrying it away off the thing's face.

I was lightheaded, felt dizzy, and fell to my knees wanting to throw up. It now towered over me, holding my hair. I was weak, sickened by what was happening, remembering something I didn't want to.

The bones of this thing cracked and cricked—deafening over the birds, the body didn't move, but the head of the thing slid underneath my hanging head. Touching forehead to forehead, I had no choice but to stare into the white centers of this thing's eyes. Harnessing the last bit of energy that I could, I swung the hammer, smashing it into my own head.

I awoke rolling off my bed onto the floor. I stayed on the floor, staring directly at the ceiling. The swaying shadows of the branches danced for me. Music played from my phone, telling me it was morning. It was still so dark outside that it didn't feel like morning. Sitting up, I let my hands glide against my room's carpet, each fluffy bristle running through my hands like reeds from growing grain. I lifted myself up onto my bed, grabbed my phone, and shut off the alarm. I lay back down, laying my head softly onto my pillow. I ran my hands underneath the pillow, and in the middle held in both hands, was a hammer.

CHAPTER 8

GOING DEEPER

KORD

I froze up when the rocks shuffled this time—it broke the sound of trickling water. My head snapped to attention in the direction of the noise. A long corridor illuminated only by a single stream of light from a flashlight that got more intense as it got ever closer. I squinted and lifted my hand to block part of the light. It was Raef. The trickling water continued.

"I can tell you the days of when I was a child, and I'd sit down in the family den listening to my grandfather and grandmother play a viola and piano. The days were getting shorter then, in the fall, and the scarecrow in our little garden was hard at work letting birds eat our fall produce. But, alas, the music from my grandparents was able to take away almost all pain and stress. It was a simple and blissful peace.

"This is not one of those times," I said.

"Oh? Why is that Kord?" Raef said, getting close enough that his flashlight could let him fully see the situation.

"No sirree, nothing like getting caught with yourself fully out and vulnerable while taking a piss," I said at slightly louder pitch.

"Dear Lord," Raef muttered, turning away from me.

I then finished. Cleared my throat. Zipped up my pants. And braced myself for the ever-inevitable dribble that happens no matter how much you shake it out.

"What? You're the one that walked in on me," I said.

"You're the one that ran off."

"What ya mean?"

"One second you were asking me a question, and the next you were gone."

"Raef, I didn't move."

"Uh-huh. Well, we're moving now, Kord."

"Where to, boss?"

Raef took out his map and flipped it every which way in an attempt to orientate it. Each fold and turn was snappier than the last. He seemed to make his gaze deliberately avert mine.

"Alright, we're going to need to head this way," Raef said, pointing and taking a step.

"Oy, isn't that the way we came?" I asked, getting in his path.

"Indeed, it is, but there's another possible passage. It's just going to take a good bit of walking."

"How long y'all talking?" I asked while crossing my arms.

"Honestly, no idea," Raef said and shook his head.

I didn't have much of a choice to listen to him, now did I? I didn't know this man, other than what he had told me, and I didn't have much else to lose at this point. Lost in a cave with my mind running wild and a stranger who just saw me peeing—I swore it couldn't get any worse.

But then it got worse. As we backtracked, we kept going down—every so often we'd face a decline or a small ledge that you'd have to sit and slide off of like a school bus evacuation. We didn't speak a word to each other for what could've been an hour or just a couple minutes. It's not like I didn't try to, but whenever I commented on something, he'd grunt, and when I asked a question, he'd just keep silent. I just chalked it up to the fact he saw me exposed and draining the lizard.

Raef was silent, barely spoke, and even his movements didn't make a noise.

There was this large open room, for lack of a better term, that we entered. It felt like we were entering some type of terminal or network hub at a station. The cave floor beneath us turned from solid rock to a mushy, foul smelling sludge. It wasn't deep, but it made a squishy sound like overly moist mac and cheese. I immediately missed the silence. Not because of the mac and cheese floor, but because of a lone droning hum. That damn humming.

"If this floor isn't the cringiest sound that I've ev—" I started to say, but then bumped into Raef.

He had stopped in front of me, his back straight. His flashlight illuminated a large symbol on the cave wall. Raef snapped his head from the map to the wall, back to the map, then back to the wall, and two glances left and right as if crossing the road. He was ignoring the hum or couldn't hear it. He bent down and scooped up part of the floor. A viscous, clumpy mush ran like sewage from his hand, not even leaving a film or slime behind on his hand either. It wasn't hard, it wasn't solid, and it didn't look heavy, but it sounded like clay bricks hitting the floor.

The humming grew louder, and Raef couldn't pretend anymore. He turned to face me.

"Kord, do you have any matches?"

"Uh, yeah," I said and turned around. "Smallest pocket. There'll be a small box of weatherproof matches."

He yanked and tugged on the pack. The zipper never budged or opened.

"Easy! You're going to break off the damn thing!"

"I cannot find them."

"You didn't even open the—oh let me do it."

I whipped my backpack around to my front, unzipped the front pocket with ease, took out the matchbox, then zipped it back up.

Raef gave me a blank stare and took the matches. He struck a match and placed it against the symbol. I was in awe, my mouth agape as the fire traced out a large circle on the wall. At six points, the fire went in different, straight directions toward other points of the circle, but they never connected.

Raef made a guttural sound and walked back toward me.

"What's that all about?" I asked him.

He reached down into the weird muck and lifted an odd-looking stick. It was one of those sticks you find as a kid in your back yard or in the park that is perfectly straight with one hole in the middle of it. He took out an oversized handkerchief, presumably for his oversized nose, wrapped it around that odd stick, and lit it on fire. The match went out.

"Raef, y'all got a flashlight. Why do you need a tor—"

Again, he didn't answer. Instead, he just nodded in a single direction and spear chucked the torch down a corridor. It lit up in an atomic fury. We were a good twenty or so meters away, but still, the flames and heat licked against our bodies. Raef smiled and even let out a little laugh as the corridor kept burning.

"Spider webs. Nasty, sticky things." Raef said.

"How did you know that?"

He pointed his flashlight back to the wall and said, "The symbol there is just letting us know that these ways here are the right direction, but they have spiders in them. All of them."

Again, I was left unanswered. The lines on the wall had connected themselves, and the humming grew louder.

"Can you stop being so cryptic, Raef? Why are there symbols all around? I can understand the numbers and shit, but this?" I got louder with each question, using my whole body to speak.

Raef paid me no attention.

"Raef. Just one answer is all I ask. Look, look, look. Numbers and letters together? Sure, alright, makes perfect sense to me. Going down to come up to another exit? Okay. A chamber with a giant Star of David shining by fire, and spider webs around us? What? Why? Just answer one of those!"

Raef put a hand on my shoulder, his eyes wide.

"Kord, we have to get moving."

"Why?"

He started dragging me with him and said, "We just do."

"No! Not until you give me an answer or a damn good reason."

Raef pointed with a stiff, unmoving, unshaking arm. I followed it from his shoulder, to the tip of his finger, and to the subject he was drawing attention to.

We had dropped down into this room, and in the ledge side was another entrance. And in front of that entrance stood that white face again. It tilted its head at us, staying still. It tilted it the other way and started toward us. As it did, the humming grew louder again.

"Come on, Kord!" Raef dashed down the corridor, the sloshing muck turning back into hard rock.

I stumbled and fell at the entrance of the corridor. That thing looked down at me, almost as if it were sorry for me. It then looked down the corridor toward Raef. I looked back at Raef, who mouthed "I'm sorry" and continued like a dog with its tail between its legs. The thing did not chase him. Instead, it looked back down at me, and I scurried back on my hands into the corridor.

Being this close to it with better lighting, I was caught in a trance with this thing's eyes. They were not blank at all as I first thought. They were eggshell in color and cloudy with a blueish tint. Inside these blue clouds were small black dots, like pupils, that had different jagged pieces like a broken window that didn't shatter, and each jagged piece mirrored everything it saw.

The trance was sad; it felt like a lifetime. I have no better way to describe it than it was like feeling a tearing pain I hadn't felt since I was tossed from a car and awoke in farm grass on a rainy night. The trance was broken when its skeletal hand reached for me. Again, I got a better look at the features of this thing. The hand had a faint hint at having skin at one point—it was leathery and wrinkled, and shards of dulled glass protruded from it.

Kord. It didn't say it, and yet I heard it.

I scurried to my feet, keeping my eyes on it, flashlight in hand, and ran. "Raef!"

A wave of déjà vu washed over me as I ducked and dove through the rocks. I didn't pay attention. Then something stopped me. I was tugged on, by what I will never know. But I'm glad it did, for right in front of me was a person lying up against the wall, their eyes closed, almost familiar. On the ground next to them was a flare gun. I knelt down next to them, keeping my eyes right on them. The mouth hung open, face skinny as all hell. I carefully grabbed the gun and inspected it. It was loaded.

There was a grunt. My eyes bugged out, and I slowly tilted my head up to meet face to face with a pair of wide, dilated, bloodshot eyes. Both of our sweat was cold, and his was thicker on the skin than mine was. The brush of their hair against mine sent a wave of uneasy chills down my spine. Neither of us moved for a solid minute. I think his eyes were hazel at one point, but the irises were not easy to make out in low lighting. They smacked their lips, and a short, dry tongue poked from their mouth.

They grabbed for me with a lightning speed I thought I wouldn't match, and yet I did. I was quicker. The flare gun in their mouth, my finger on the trigger. I must have pulled it, because they lit up in a spectacular blaze and fell off of me. Burning up and flailing about, still trying to grab for me, the flames melted their body and blood ran down the arms and hands. The arms fell off as they just kept screaming. And screaming. And screaming. I closed my eyes and clamped my ears.

"Shut up! Shut up, shut up, shut up!" I screamed.

But they didn't listen, if they even wanted to, they couldn't. I cried. Couldn't help it.

"A-aa…" they slurred.

"N-no. This isn't happening…" I stammered, slapping myself on each syllable.

Screaming. There was still screaming. I stopped slapping myself, because by this point, I didn't know what was a dream and what wasn't, and even if I did, I couldn't snap out of it. I held my ears again, trying to shield them from the pain. I watched. I watched. And I watched.

And then I recognized him. *He* screamed the same way *she* did. I don't know what started shaking first, my hands or my head. But it felt like a rolling pin was crushing my guts, and that someone had taken a mixer to my head. It eventually was as if my entire body was thrown into a pressure cooker.

GOING DEEPER · 79

The smell invaded my senses. I could practically taste the smell from the burning guy.

"Raef... Raef," I slurred, spitting it out between my shaking, trying to keep myself from turning inside out via my mouth.

Footsteps from someone flatfooted came from the corridor behind me. They grew closer and closer, and something hit me like a horse at full gallop. I hit the ground with what felt like the force of falling from a cliff.

It was vile. Not just what was coming out of my mouth, but what was going through my mind. I tried to push out as much as I could, and while it would eventually reemerge with a vengeance, it lost the battle for now. I took one last look at the smoldering guy, his screaming died down, presumably as he started dying down. I slumped down right next to him.

"Kord? Kord!" The darkness said, closing in around me.

With a darkness like coal, and the beating of my heart thudding against my ear drums, sounding like maracas, the darkness hummed and asked, *Why, Kord?*

* * *

I was alone. In a vast sea of fog. I looked around me to see nothing but several bodies of myself walking around, minding their own business. A thunderous crack roared from behind me. I put my hands to my ears, not because they hurt, but because they didn't. They bled onto my hands, but perhaps for my own good.

I turned to a black-robed figure approaching me and quick. I couldn't run, for I couldn't move my feet. I couldn't speak, for my voice felt like it was stripped. I looked to my blood-stained hands. And I wiped my hand across my forehead, smearing my own blood onto it. I rolled back my shoulders and watched as a viscous burgundy replaced the fog.

"Kord," Raef said. "Kord."

I clenched my eyes tighter before opening them. Raef was sitting across from me, his back against the opposite wall. I moved myself to sit up, groaning as I did.

"Have a nice nap?"

"Uh-huh," I said through gritted teeth.

"You okay?"

"Maybe. How long was I out for?" I asked, laying my head against the wall.

"Ten minutes, perhaps. You make a friend?" Raef said, motioning to the body.

"You're disgusting, you know that? Why couldn't the Game Commission or whoever send somebody normal?" I said, looking back to the body.

I tightened my lips, raised my eyebrows, and again felt like I was an ingredient to something. He laid motionless, face down, on the ground. There was no smell. There was no smoke. There was no fiery light. And there were two arms still attached to them. I popped open the flare gun, and it still had its cartridge in it. Clear as day, from some light above shining upon it, was a large emblem with the words "PA SEARCH AND RESCUE." I turned away and hung my head.

A soft tap hit the top of my head. I tilted it slowly, ready to accept anything. A soft tap hit my face. Directly above me and the deceased, maybe fifty meters or so, was a decent sized hole. The sky greeted me with gray and black, and the wind said hello with its hallowed howling, and a red flag, lit up by a small light from somewhere above, spasmed in the wind. Also lit up by the light was a rope ladder, that was broken about halfway down the hole.

CHAPTER 9

INCIDENT REPORT

MAYOR SMITT

I dropped my desk phone, not on the receiver, but just to wherever it fell. I ran out of my office and stopped at my aid's desk, leaning over it, looking into her surprised eyes, out of breath.

"Ay, Pana! I do not know how to properly describe my intrigue, nervousness, and overall frustration about the current situation. Clarkson and Theresa Sherman came to see me at my home, and after hearing of the trouble Kord was in, I had to take report of and pronto.

"Their description of inside sends chills down my side—a marionette, cassette, inscriptions? Take a look at what I sent out," I said, handing a short and brief report to my aid, "And guess whom I just got off the phone with."

"I dunno, what? Wait, marionette? The fuck? 'Scuse my language, ma'am," the aid responded.

"I know, right? Creepy as hell, and don't worry about it. But, no, um, yeah. I just got off the phone with the National Park Service. I was in contact with them after I submitted that report. They call me. Ask for *my* name, and then the line goes absolutely silent for a good few seconds, and I end up talking with this guy who only identified as 'Mr. Martin.' That's all who I'm getting."

"What did he ask you?" my aid asked, absolutely bewildered.

"Almost nothing. He asked who I was. He asked me about who was in the cave. He asked about any more carvings, and he asked if just the two got out. He was so fervent to know."

"That's odd."

"He finished with asking if I was afraid. I said no, but I was worried about this young man's safety. He told me to assume the absolute worst."

"Why the absolute worst? Who the hell does that guy think he is?"

"Ay bendito. I don't know. Some gringo is all I can think of. He didn't sound important."

"What's 'Green-go'?"

I shook my head, covering my mouth, "Oh, just slang. Don't worry about it."

"Uh-huh," my aid said. "Well take a looky-looky at this. It came in half an hour ago. I was going to hand it off, but he said to hand it directly to you."

I closed my eyes and sighed, putting out my hand. She put a manila envelope in my hand, the ones with the red string to wrap around the back of it, upside down. I could tell the type, because these envelopes had a rougher texture versus a smoother envelope that had the metal prongs. It contained one piece of paper, and I could tell because one piece of paper could still shift around inside and make a scratching noise. Two pieces were more like a light rubbing and so on.

I flipped it over. I gave my aid an offending look. I didn't mean to, but I had had enough for one day.

"From Lieutenant Governor Meyer, huh?" I asked.

"'Tis who it is from," my aid said, crossing her arms.

I started to unwrap the string.

"No, no. He said to read it in your office. Door closed. Blinds down. And don't let the document face any reflective surfaces. Most importantly, he said, and I quote, 'For God's sake, turn all of the lights *on*.'"

I huffed, rolled my eyes, and went to my office. On my walk back, several things rushed through my mind about what this was. I thought that he might've been coming for a visit to the local college, but that wouldn't be as confidential. In fact, that would be public. I thought about the roads: I-81 and the Turnpike I-76; Routes 11, 74, 34, et cetera, et cetera. But I shoved that aside, too. Even if it was anything about the podium toppling discussions happening in Harrisburg, that were helping Meyer in making many "friends," became absent from my mind.

I was hypervigilant of the paintings on the walls, looking at them as they looked at me. Looking out the windows into the approaching dusk, and the dusk seeming to grow closer to me more than anywhere else, for once in my life, since I was a kid on *Borikén*—Puerto Rico—I was scared. Truly fearful, for what, I did not know.

The moment I got back into my office, I closed and locked the door. I tossed the envelope onto my desk, pulling down the blinds on each window in my office. In addition, I pulled the two layers of blackout curtains shut over the windows looking outside. I flicked on every switch and turned on every lamp. I went back to my desk.

I picked up the envelope and started unwinding it quickly. I slowed, as my eyes were attracted to the map on my desk. It was dull in color—mostly blacks and tans, plus little bits of greens, yellows, blues, and reds—but was not dull in the emotion behind it. Not right now. It was of the known cave systems in the area. I sighed and opened the envelope. It read:

Mayor Smitt,

Martin does not know everything. His tobacco covered tongue is more silver than the one who possesses the silver tongue. Look for the orange ink at the top of the map on your desk. Tell no one of this. Have a nice day!

Meyer

Normally, my mind would have probably raced, but it was empty. I put down the letter with a pair of vibrating hands. I scanned my eyes across the top of the map. Indeed, in a faint and wet orange ink was "Kord" with an arrow pointing up off of the map.

CHAPTER 10

THE LIEUTENANT GOVERNOR

CLARKSON

I got the message over the radio. Cops had been sent to the cave entrance, but they had not had any reply from Kord. I was heartbroken but resolved to do something now more than ever. I was scared at first, too, because the other two parties asked why there was so much static. Overdid it a bit on my end. No matter. They blamed it on the weather. But it was clear…

I had to tell Theresa. We had to do something. I was not about to sit here any longer just doing nothing, not like I had been these past two days or even before. I poked my head out from the door, looking up and down the hallway for her. I then looked to the seat where she thinks that being so still means she won't be noticed. The cat waddled past, flopping its little feet, meowing without a care in the world. I snapped my head directly at Theresa. It spooked her.

"You think you're so invisible over there, don't ya?" I asked.

"Never said that," she said.

"Not verbally, mind you. Anyways, come in here, I need you to see something."

She tilted her head with the most perplexed look on her face, then asked, "What's up, Clark?"

She got up, letting the rocking chair squeak as it always does. I closed the door behind her and handed her a piece of paper with rudely scribbled words and abbreviations on it that I had labeled a transcript. She read it over, looked to me, and read it again. She handed it back slowly, hanging her head, and sat on my bed.

"Okay, well. We can't give up hope, bro. Remember, Smitt wants us to come in tomorrow to talk with that guy from the NPS."

"I'm not. And I know, but he's a Fed. We need to actually do something, sis." I sat next to her.

"Ye, but what?"

"I don't know," I enthusiastically said in disappointment.

We thought for a minute. Sitting there, the cat's collar bell jingling as it thudded down the stairs shaking the house, was the only sound. Then my beauty of machinery and radio technology came to life and talked to us. It was all static at first, and I don't think it was any one specific conversation, but from it came "Meyer" in broken-up pieces. I looked to Theresa.

"What did that say?" she asked, pointing at it.

"I believe it just told us Meyer," I answered.

"Lieutenant Governor Meyer?"

"Do you know any others?"

She looked at it, then to me. She shook her head and stood.

"Look, sis, it's probably a good idea anyways. I mean, come on. He's popular among all of the state. Hell, even the Prime Minister of Japan asked to visit him when he was in

DC. He's uncouth, but he's fair and moral. He'll be more than willing to help, I bet."

She held herself, shrugging her shoulders, and said, "Look, yeah. I know. Under any other circumstance I would think that a flawless thing to do, it wouldn't hurt then. But. But. But that thing was off when you brought me in here, and it turned on, saying his name in broken conversation, like a spirit box. I don't know. That doesn't sit well with me, bro. I-I-I-I don't like it with how that was suggested."

I thought for a second and said, "What if it was Dad trying to help?"

"That's a big 'if' Clark."

"Still, I didn't have it fully off. It's just not tuned to anything specific."

She looked at me with large puppy dog eyes, looking at me then the radio and back again. She sighed and nodded.

"Alright, okay. Fine, but don't we have to call him and set an appointment or something?" she asked.

"Or, we could just drive up and catch him during his off hours in the backyard," I suggested.

"Clark. How do you know that?"

"It was in the paper earlier. The guy was out in the back yard, tending to his blueberry bush, and he found this giant vole, like nearly ten inches long, and—" I said and looked up at my sister who still wasn't any surer of the idea. I took out my phone, getting back to the point, "—and he would be out there till dusk most likely. Besides, he hasn't taken residence at the usual place in Indiantown Gap. He's renting a house on the river near that train shop big sis liked, just over in New Cumberland."

"You talkin' about the one near the middle school?"

"Yeah! Dat one."

Theresa groaned. "Well…I guess, Clark."

I beamed at her, and she curled the corner of her lips softly.

* * *

Theresa and I pulled up to the residence. It had beige brick on the outside with a white roof. Two windows flanked the door, and two smaller windows flanked those. The front patio was small, with a covering that came out about five feet from the house. The driveway was big enough to fit two cars side by side and had two garage doors. There was an aspen tree just outside by the reddish-brown stained fence. We parked on the street and walked around the side of the house to the back yard. We peered around the corner of the house, and he was gardening. He stood up and wiped away the sweat from his square face. He wore beat-up jeans and an old torn-up white tee that showed a well-kept but not trained figure.

"Oh man," Theresa whispered.

"What?" I asked.

"He's kinda hot."

"Theresa, he is a *lot* older than you," I said, looking at her.

"So was Mom to Dad. Six years difference," she said, looking back.

"He is sixteen years your senior."

"And I can hear you," Meyer said, looking directly at us, "Can I help you two?"

He wiped dirt from his hands, grabbed his water, and walked over to us. He held out a finger, chugged some water and let down his finger.

"*Ah*, that went down the wrong pipe. Excuse my dirtiness, but, you know, this is my property," he said. His voice was deep and had a barely noticeable rasp.

"Uhhhhhhh," Theresa and I said in unison.

He stared at us, waiting for an answer. I cleared my throat and shook my head.

"Oh, uh, yeah. My name is Clarkson Sherman, and this is my sister, Theresa Sherman. We have a problem we were hoping you could help with."

"Does it involve an expedition or looking out the car window at a deer, Clarkson?"

"No. Well, I'm not expecting it too."

"Good. Then I might be able to help. Meet me inside. Just walk through the front door, and I'll… Is your sister okay?"

"Uhhhh." Theresa was still making a quiet noise.

"She will be," I answered.

I snapped Theresa from her trance, and we met Meyer in his house.

"Anything to drink, you two? Water or tea? Coffee?" Meyer asked.

"Just water for us," I said.

He turned to Theresa. "Is that good for you, Miss Sherman?"

She nodded vigorously.

He sat down at the small wooden table, putting the water down in front of us. He cracked open a Yuengling and sipped it. The house on the inside was nothing special. Pretty bare, with some decoration. It was clear that he spent more time tending to outdoor appearances than inside.

"So, what seems to be the issue? Taxes? Education?" he asked.

"It's about our friend Kord," I said.

Theresa sipped on her water loudly.

Meyer looked to her then back to me. "What happened? Is he okay?" He took a sip.

"He's kinda…trapped in a cave," I said.

Meyer nearly choked on his beer and looked at me then at Theresa.

I sipped my water. "It's the truth."

"Stuck in a cave?"

"Ya, sir," Theresa said.

"Damn, I didn't think—" Meyer's voice trailed off. "Okay, is it over on the Conodoguinet?" he asked.

"Um, yeah. How did…" I said.

"I got a copy of the report this morning from Mayor Smitt. I'm sorry to hear about your friend," he said then asked, "Did you by chance catch who they're sending from Fed to help?"

He looked directly at me. He half smiled and then dropped it.

"Some guy named Mr. Martin," I said.

"God dammit! I thought you would say that," Meyer said, pounding his fist on the table.

"You know him?" Theresa asked.

"Yeah. We go back. Maybe more than any two people should. Just dealing with Fed intervention isn't fun. We'll leave it at that," he said and winked at the end.

"Not a fan of the Fed myself," I said.

Meyer gave a half-hearted chuckle to that. "Is that so?"

"Are you in here alone?" Theresa asked.

Meyer and I looked at her with caution, both leaning away from her. Her expression had gone from her head being in the clouds to being back down to earth, back down to business.

"Yes, I am," he answered.

"Good," Theresa started, and I began to say something before she stopped me. "We want to help in getting him out, but there's not a whole lot that we can really do, ya know?"

Meyer nodded. "I think I understand what you're saying. Are you going to ask me to share with you stuff I'm not supposed to?"

"I am not asking that. I am going to say that any way you are able to help will be highly obliged," Theresa said with a wink.

I felt completely left out, but at least Theresa was speaking again. Meyer smirked, nodded, and chortled.

"I'll be right back," Meyer said and left the table.

I watched him walk upstairs and turned back to Theresa. She sipped her water loudly, shooting me a quick glance. After a short bit, Meyer returned to the table with something in his hands. We stood since he was still standing.

"Theresa, take this. It is a burner phone. There is no caller ID on it. I will call you twice in a row. Only pick up on the second call. Never pick up on the first call. I don't know how often we'll need it, probably not much, but it's a good way of contact. You two do what you can. When you find and meet Mr. Martin, if you ever do, let me know anything about him you pick up on. I'll do what I can here. This must be hush, hush. Understood?"

Theresa and I nodded. He smiled and motioned for the door. He followed us out, holding the door for us. I looked out the window of the car and saw Meyer walking in front of his window, looking into the corner, seemingly talking to nothing.

CHAPTER 11

MR. MARTIN

CLARKSON

The building was old, but not outdated. The desires of the old colonial and post-colonial appearance and layout of the town usually gave Carlisle its homey feeling, but right now I only felt trapped. And for the few times that I had been inside this building, I had never been inside Mayor Smitt's office this much until this whole Shakespearean tragedy. Theresa and I are locked outside the castle that holds the party.

Theresa told me that this room is usually bright, warm, cheerful, yadda yadda yadda. Whether or not that has any truth behind it, it surely ain't so now. Whatever light used to shine through those drapes, the curtains, the blinds on these windows mock us. Gray storm clouds laugh at us from the road on high, ready to spit on us. Whatever comfort there was to these executive chairs, with all their cushioning and padding and all their soft, clean upholstery, now only stuck and sealed us like glue.

I swung my feet, unable to touch the floor, and gripped the armrests of my chair as I spun around in it. Theresa told me that I was drumming my fingers on the chair's wood frame. Rolling my fingers like a horse's gallop. I do not remember doing this, nor much of what we talked about in the office, but I trust her memory.

"Clark, calm down," Theresa said, speaking softly. She was sitting in the chair next to me.

"How, why?"

"You can start by not thumbing the chair arm like a rabbit."

"Look, fine, okay?" I crossed my arms. "I'm relaxed. No thumbin'. Just chillin'. No worry here."

"Clark, bro—"

"Calm. Calm, calm, calm. Totally calm," I lied, waving my hands and bouncing my leg.

"Clarkson," Theresa said and put her hand on my knee. "Calm. Down. Kord will be fine, and we're going to help him, okay?"

"Okay? How can I be okay? My best friend, since I was shitting my pants being scared, is stuck in a goddamned cave of all places," I said.

I stood from my chair and began to pace. I had pushed the chair away from me with more force than I had ever intended, it flung back into the wall and broke a bit of the drywall. I cringed upon hearing the cracking sound and ground my teeth like they were was metal grinders.

"Clarkson!"

"What?"

"Being upset is one thing. You think I'm not?" She tapped her chest with a knife-hand. "I'm worried sick about him, too, and in case you've forgotten, he's my friend as well."

What I did next, I hope I am remembering incorrectly, for I wish it to have never happened. I had approached my sister, got my finger in her face, and felt an anger rising inside me that made more than my face turn red. My blood rushed around, fogging my judgement and my mind in general. I was shaking, to the extent that I was unable to hold my finger still. It curled ever so slowly, almost into a fist. My sight grew blurry and my cheeks wet. I turned from my sister, took in a long deep breath, held it, and let it out.

I walked back over to my chair, grabbed it, and pushed it back into place. Before I sat down in it, I moved an office plant just enough to cover the hole and not draw suspicion.

Clarkson, you bastard, you're only making more trouble for yourself, I thought.

But you're justified, something else thought for me.

I shook my head clear and slunk down in the chair. I looked toward Theresa.

"I'm sorry," I said.

"I know you are," she replied.

We sat there, not speaking to one another, the only sound being from the buzzing air conditioner, vibrating vents, and the swaying plastic grips at the end of the blinds' pull cords tapping against the drywall. A clacking of shoes broke the tension in the air. One set was undoubtedly Ms. Smitt's heavy-heeled shoes, every clack sounding like she was marching. I didn't recognize the second set. It was softer, but that doesn't really mean too much if I'm honest. It sounded almost as if the soles of the shoes had wood on them, like clogs. Two shadows passed along the blinds on the windows looking into the hallway. One short one, Ms. Smitt, and one tall shadow that seemed to linger more than it should've.

The door opened. In walked Ms. Smitt and following behind her was the owner of the second shadow.

A tall, skinny man with short, curly, brown hair and a hint at sideburns wore a light brown blazer over a white cotton button-up, a gray tie, and a pair of stiff, denim jeans. In addition to the odd fashion choices of the man, he had a squared-off jawline on an otherwise oval head, evenly stubbled facial hair, and a squashed, almost flat nose with nostrils that stuck out, making it look like there was an arrow pointing down his face. His eyes were almost almonds: they were rounded closer to the bridge of his nose, but quickly became angled and sloped down into squinty corners akin to those found on a tired elderly man.

He carried with him a beat-up, brown leather briefcase and walked tall, proud, with meaning, like that you'd find from George C. Scott in his portrayal of Patton, but he followed Ms. Smitt. Before they sat down, Smitt pulled the chair out for this tall mystery man, and he sat down in it, lightly grabbed Ms. Smitt's hand, and thanked her like she was his own mother. Smitt smiled and sat down shortly after.

The man put his briefcase on the table but did not open it, instead taking out a notepad and pen from his blazer's inner pocket. He wrote a few things down. And so, for almost a minute, we sat across from each other at this rectangular polished oak table. Theresa and I on one side, our backs to the windows looking outside, and Ms. Smitt and the man with their backs facing the windows to the hallway.

"Theresa, Clarkson," Smitt started, nodding to both of us in the order she spoke, "this is Mr. Martin, the gentleman I told you both about who is here from the National Park Service to talk with you both."

"Miss Sherman. Master Sherman." His voice was soft and a bit raspy. He shook both of our hands. "I'm willing to assume that both of you want to know *why* I am here and not just the 'what.' Would that be a fair assumption?"

Theresa and I nodded.

"I was wondering more why you look like you're from the early 2000s," Theresa said, trying to clear the air.

"'Cause I'm comfortable, that's why," he said, shifting in his seat and leaning on the table. "I'm here to help conduct an investigation into the disappearance of your friend Kord. I have been filled in on the basics so far. You were in a cave, an off-limits one at that, and inside, your friend Kord was trapped by some falling rock. Is there anything I missed?"

"He was trapped behind the rock, not in the rock," Theresa said. "And—"

"And inside there were some odd objects that seemed out of place," Mr. Martin said.

Again, Theresa and I nodded.

"I have to warn you two. You're in something deeper than you think. And *that*, Mayor Smitt, is off the record," he said, raising one finger while still looking at us.

Mayor Smitt huffed softly and moved her eyes from Mr. Martin, to the table, to us. She and I made eye contact, and for as much as she tried, she was unable to hold eye contact with me.

"Now, for on the record, walk me through the course of the day and day before. What did y'all do?" Mr. Martin asked, taking pen to pad.

"Well…" Theresa started.

She continued to talk, but I stopped paying attention, having my mind become more preoccupied by my thoughts. An inner monologue if you will. I kept blaming myself, for everything that was happening. How could I not? I organized it all. Kept telling myself to "never mind this" and "never mind that."

It wasn't just another little adventure, I told myself. *It wasn't Indian Echo Caverns. Nothing was preplanned. Nothing was already mapped. Nothing was—*"

"And what about you, Master Sherman? May I call you by your first name?" Mr. Martin asked me.

"Oh, huh? Uh, um, yeah, you can. Clarkson," I said, sitting back up right.

"In that case, Clarkson, would you agree with the order of events that your sister described?"

"Sure, I guess. I'll be honest, I wasn't paying too much attention. Her memory is better than mine, anyways."

"I see."

Mr. Martin leaned back in his chair and opened the opposite side of the blazer that the pen and notepad had been in. He pulled out a small glass jar with latches on each side of the lid and a rubber seal. It was clean for now. He then took out a silver thing. He opened it and took out a cigarette and tapped the top of it against the closed silver thing three times. Taking out a lighter and putting the cigarette up to his lips, he kept his eyes on me.

Mr. Martin took a long drag of the cigarette and took it away from his lips. The smoke escaped from the corners of his mouth and his nostrils like a dragon. He nodded his head slowly, as if to a beat. He opened the small glass jar and flicked the ash from the end of the cigarette into it. He took another long drag, longer than the first. He let it out regularly this time, with a sigh. He looked to the jar as he flicked the ashes from it a second time.

"Now, Clarkson. I do believe you when you say you weren't paying attention. And I believe you when you say that your sister has a better memory than you do. Honest to Jehovah. Say what you will of the stereotype that women have better memories than men, to a degree I accept that as a fact, but the true reason I believe you is because your sister was able to remember the color of her pancakes. Now, Clarkson. Something else is on your mind."

He put his eyes back onto mine. He looked into me. Not at me, not through me, into me. I felt uncomfortable, but I would not let myself show it. I stiffened my back and leaned onto the table toward Mr. Martin. He mirrored me and leaned in.

"What do you want to know?" I asked calmly.

"Just. What. Is. On. Your." He took a shorter drag. "Mind."

"You already know, don't you?"

The smoke escaped from his lips, blowing it out softly, almost right at me.

"Maybe," he said.

"Tuff shit, Fed-boy."

"Clark," Theresa said, uneased, pushing me back into my seat.

Mr. Martin kept his eyes on me and then leaned back into his seat. He chatted his teeth together, sliding his jaw back and forth. He looked to his notepad, picked up the pen, and wrote something down. For some reason, that set me off.

"Do you want to know his grades too? He usually got low As high Bs, not hard at his school of some thousand kids. Just exist and show up for class for a grade. His favorite subject was history. He likes to read graphic novels, watch cartoons and old TV shows. Kord'll usually walk around with a pair of dark blue dress shoes. He's got short hair that he gets trimmed every week by his grandfather. He doesn't drive. He doesn't smoke. Doesn't drink. Doesn't fight. Hell, I'll bet that that bastard doesn't even touch himself!"

Ms. Smitt widened her eyes, and Mr. Martin's eyebrows levitated up his forehead. They exchanged looks.

"Clark!" Theresa slapped me across the face, leaving a large red mark on my cheek.

I ignored the searing redness, keeping my eyes on Mr. Martin, "If you're trying to test me to see if I truly do know him, then now you best damn know. Want his birthday? October 6, 2004. His eye color? Brown, but they're darker in the winter. Height? He's five-feet, six inches, taller than my short four-foot-eleven ass. Now," I stood up to lean across the table, "what else do you want to know, asshole?"

Mr. Martin leaned back in his chair, leaning back as far as the chair would allow before lifting off the ground. He looked me up and down, pursing his lips and rocking his head. He leaned back forward.

"Clarkson, I do believe I must've done something to offend you. That or you have an insatiable Napoleon complex."

"Napoleon wasn't even that short! He was average height. French inches were bigger than English inches," I rattled off the tongue like it was muscle memory. My hands did as much talking as my mouth, flailing about without much care.

"Is that what you tell the ladies?"

"Mr. Martin," Ms. Smitt said with a tone that hit like a blacksmith's hammer on metal.

Mr. Martin just shrugged his shoulders, keeping his eyes on me.

"Theresa, I ask that you excuse me if I angered your Corsican brother. And Ms. Smitt, I do believe that this is a good time for us to excuse ourselves. I got all I'll get from the two. Either from willingness or from frustration," Mr. Martin said.

"Please, excuse Clarkson, he's—" Theresa was saying.

"He's untrusting of the Fed. I understand. It's not the first time."

Mr. Martin put his cigarette into the glass jar, latched it, and put it into his blazer pocket. He did the same to the pen and notepad, putting them away. He stood up, pushed in his chair, and picked up the briefcase.

"You said he still lives with his grandparents, correct Theresa?" he asked.

"Yes."

"Very well. Perhaps they have something that could help me. Does that sound like an okay idea, Ms. Smitt?" he said, looking at the table, almost lost in thought.

"Y-yes, we could do that."

"Good. Since this is the main administrative building of the city, you're bound to have records on the inhabitants of the city limits, no? I'd like to see it," he said before Ms. Smitt could respond.

Ms. Smitt simply nodded and started for the door.

"And one more thing, Clarkson. Tell Meyer 'yes.' This is still his old gray tie. The bastard's bound to know," Mr. Martin said and stormed from the room.

Ms. Smitt looked shocked at Mr. Martin as he left and then back to us. She looked like she was about to say something but didn't and ran after Mr. Martin. Theresa and I were free to go, we knew, but we sat motionless for an eternity. Theresa finally stood and walked over to the window. About a minute passed and she waved.

"Something is not right, Clark."

"I know."

There was another brief silence. I hung my head and cursed myself under my breath, and as quiet as I tried to be, Theresa heard me.

"Stop beating yourself up. I know you are, bro."

"Tell me all you want; it's still going to happen. I can only imagine the fun he's having right now."

A patter of rain rolled like snare drums against the window.

CHAPTER 12

IN THE SENATE

MEYER

The clouds for a few days had been growing darker and darker. Two storms for one. One would think that they were bringing misery and pain for everybody, but in reality, one will overpower the other, leaving one storm. That's not to say the weaker of the two won't do any damage, but in some ways, the larger undoes the damage of the weaker.

Now if only that could've saved me from the shitshow I was in. Also known as politics.

* * *

Not too long ago, there was a minor debacle involving a certain building in this country. Since then, reds have been on the decline, braking from one another like the other reds did. A weird Pan-American mix arose across the lands from Anchorage to Miami and Veracruz to Montreal. As more and more of the old guard faded into the background or ground itself, the young guard took the reins. I am grouped into this young guard, all because the governor is just barely old enough to hold the title of the office.

This young governor has taken near-tyrannical steps, and I have been the one getting the brunt of most of it, stepping in when she would want to storm from her office into the House. In the first set of months after being elected, she forced through bills like she was writing out receipts at a restaurant.

The first thing on her chopping block had to deal with publicly elected officials' pay, making it no more than the minimum wage. Secondly, she and her posse implemented STV, rank-choice voting with each district now being a single county with two representatives for the first five thousand people plus an additional representative for every five thousand more in the House.

Why is any of this important to tell? Well, the fire and brimstone woman and those who support her, including myself to a degree, are in the minority. Any time I have to deal with someone, it's usually with the majority breathing fire down my back and trying to whip me into submission with noes; sometimes even from the young governor herself. Nevertheless, a soft, smooth tongue can usually turn that fire into water.

Fast forward to three years into this administration. The state's GDP had been hovering around the predicted GDP growth, most unemployment was fractional, and roadwork season in Pennsylvania has declined in time, making some rejoice.

There was still a problem. The US dollar had been facing deflation. Sounds good and grand, until millions of people saw smaller numbers on their paychecks. Even after trying to explain the situation, people chose not to listen. They chose to hold on to fear.

And fear held on to them. Fear was finding a way to get out.

Enter me. Speak softly and carry a big stick. A month of near mass panic gripped the country, until a certain lieutenant governor of a certain state basically told them, but in much more polite words, to "sit down and shut up."

And then came the summer season before the general election. Things have been in a status quo. And the fire had been flicking at my back for weeks. Everyone was on edge and wanting to secure their seats.

* * *

The afternoon prior, I had met with Clarkson and Theresa Sherman. Two nice youngsters. They took after their parents; Clarkson especially took after his father. I had that evening to think things over, after taking a moment to talk with my own shadow.

I walked down the familiar sidewalk of this concrete jungle, listening to the orchestrated concert that is traffic, and the guy who always plays the guitar on the steps of the capital; he has a beautiful singing voice. Rain or shine, and today was no different. Hopping up the steps, two at a time, dropping a fiver into the guy's open guitar case and getting a little tune played for me each time I do, I entered and was greeted by a class of elementary kids on a tour in the main rotunda. They all turned and looked at me, a giant among them.

These kids were in for a "treat" today. A vote was scheduled on the use of capital punishment, not too long from now, happening in the Senate. Something that my position requires me to be involved in.

I carefully moved through the crowd of children, feeling like I was in a ballroom when I had to step around kids who refused to move. I waved and smiled at each individual one. Their teachers tried to help move the kids, being frantic about it, but they continued to stare at me like curious little deer.

"Mr. Meyer," Mr. Caden, a Senate representative from York, sounded off down the hall.

"Yes?"

"You're late."

"The voting doesn't start for another half hour, and I've already been briefed."

"Check your phone."

I reached to my hip and pulled out a small flip phone from the belt case. I opened it, and a message popped down from the top telling me of five missed calls from the Mr. Caden.

"Would help if this phone ever worked when I needed it to," I said, finally getting through the quiet gaggle of kids.

I walked toward the North Chamber. My clacking footsteps echoed from the smooth tile through the high, brilliantly painted ceiling of the St. Peter's Basilica–inspired rotunda, the sound bouncing off every granite step and each piece of carefully constructed molding, being absorbed into each drop of dried paint. I straightened out my brown double-breasted suit coat and adjusted my cuffs as I approached Mr. Caden.

"Alrighty, Mr. Caden. What did my phone fail to inform me?" I asked.

Mr. Caden held a door open with his foot, his hands in his black slacks' pockets, his eyes barely keeping open. His oversized, dull hued, baby blue suit coat was crinkled around his elbows as it draped around his waist unbuttoned and wide open. His white shirt had wrinkles around the unbuttoned collar. He gestured with his head into the room. Inside, some were standing, and others were sitting around a table; all were members of our coalition, all visibly tired, all turned to see me with a small bit of relief in their eyes. Mr. Caden closed the door and walked inside.

I leaned over on a chair at the head of the table. "What is it gents and gentettes?"

"We've hit a snag, Chinkwe," Mr. Caden said. "Miss Smith."

"Meyer," she started, a representative from Erie, "we have some…news that came across our eyes earlier. Have you seen the paper this morning?"

I shrugged and shook my head. "Naw. Is it more stuff about our efforts to—"

"Take a look, sir. Ya won't believe it," Mr. Squire, from Allegheny, said while tossing me a rolled-up paper. Making no attempt to catch it, I let it bounce off of my forehead.

"Even some members from the opposition are calling it slander, but it's done damage," Miss Korcel from Centre County, said.

I stared at the rolled-up paper on the table. I scrunched up my lips and scratched my cheek. I looked around at everyone else staring at me. I sighed and picked it up, the rubber band holding it together snapping as I rolled it off. I unrolled it, unfolded it, and snapped it taunt. I cleared my throat when I read the headline with accompanying picture: "Two Kids Enter Lieutenant Governor's Residence."

I breathed in deeply and out slowly.

"The only one there that's still a kid is Sherman's son, Clarkson," the deep-voiced Mr. Ronald from Dauphin and president pro tempore of the Pennsylvania Senate said.

"Not only that, we've made it expressly clear that you were friends with their father on top of the fact that you have an open-door policy. But, nevertheless, we can all see how others are calling bullshit," the squeaky voiced Mr. Freedman, wearing a red scarf around his neck to hide his recent surgery, from Cumberland, said. "Hell, you helped out in the cub scout den that Clarkson and my own son were a part of for a while until it dissolved. But I guess that would give fuel to the wrong people if that was made public."

Mr. Caden put his hand on my shoulder.

"They got my bad side, ya know," I said, my body shaking.

"Chinkwe, it's best to not say anything right now."

"Y-y-yeah, you know what, Mr. Caden? In all due respect, shut up. I-I-I-I just came through those doors, through a group of children," I said, trying to keep my voice level.

"You know who has already made the comment, 'He always said he enjoyed children,'" Mr. Freedman said, crossing his arms.

"I knew Fecker,"—also from Cumberland—"was after my seat, but doing something like this? The f-f-f—" I stammered, stopping to put the paper down slowly. "What is wrong with that man? This looks like it's from his own damn house, too. It has to be. You can even see the crack in the window."

"Mr. Meyer, breathe, many others are asking the same question," Miss Korcel said.

"Mhm. But it still does damage. Don't it?" I asked her.

"On a brighter note, we have people that switched from the opposition to our vote today because of it," Miss Smith said.

"Because they're shallow pigs, and we all know that," I said.

The room grew warm, each person shuffled and readjusted themselves in their seats. I breathed in and out slowly. I grabbed the seat and pulled it out from under the table. I flopped down into it. I reached into my coat's breast pocket, pulling out a silver cigarette case. I smiled and huffed to myself. I spun it in my hands.

"Ya know. They brought forward to me some information about a friend of theirs," I said and started tapping the case on the table. "Their friend's name is Kord."

"Clverson?" the silent Mr. Penelope from Perry asked.
"Yes," I said.
"Nice young man. I knew his grandparents, friends of my cousin," he said, picking his teeth.
"I'm sure he is. I gave out the order earlier this morning, as y'all have of probably heard, to organize search teams up and down the Conodoguinet. They were out exploring a cave, and Kord got trapped in the cave. At least they thought. A report I got from Mayor Smitt of Carlisle tells us that the police had no contact with the boy. Furthermore, they found a hole big enough for the description of Kord to have of moved through. Since the caves are too unknown, and the rains are coming, searching the waters is our only bet right now."

I looked to each one of them, and each one of them gave me the same "I've pissed my pants" type of look. I stopped tapping the case and put it back into my coat's breast pocket. I stared down at my shoes, rocking my heels. A small glint in the dark floor vent caught my eye. Something seemed to move side to side in there, as if shaking "no." I laughed softly and turned to the rest of my cohorts in the room.

"Ya know?" I asked, turning over my hands, examining the sweaty palms, "I've felt nails go through my hands before. Completely on accident, mind you. But I've felt nails go through my hands, and my feet, and I've had my sides stabbed. I ain't Jesus, but I'm willing to be crucified on some points."

"Ye-ye," Mr. Penelope said.
"Ye-*ye*," Mr. Ronald and Freedman echoed.

Coming from the South-Centrals, I knew what they meant. Basically, agreement. I rubbed my hands together and stood, cracking my back. The PA system came on overhead, and the sweet voice of old Mrs. Conner from Crawford came through.

"All senators to the North Chamber in ten minutes. All senators. North Chamber. Ten minutes."

Everyone got up and straightened out their suit coats, slacks, and whatnot. I rocked on my feet, looking at Mr. Caden as he opened the door. So many things went through my mind at once. My heart thudded in my ears. The soft padding of the carpet in the room yielded for the tile in the hallway. I put my hands in my pockets, the paper rolled up under my arm. A bustle of people was entering the chamber, and the kids were heading for the balcony. These kids would get a treat after all. I squeezed my nose and turned, looking back into the room.

"Mr. Ronald, president pro tempore, you will preside over the vote today."

"Where are you going, Meyer?" Mr. Ronald asked me with a very worried and confused look on his face.

"Follow me and find out."

I gave him a toothy grin, goose-stepping down the hall to the chamber. They hurried to catch up to me. I started to whistle. The others followed me, presumedly confused, just how I wanted them.

I walked through the chamber doors, a small sea of people parting for me. The chamber's noise died down.

"Where's Fecker?" I asked in a calm voice, but with authority.

No one answered. I walked in a bit further. There was some clacking coming from in the hallway, sounded like security.

"Fecker?" I asked again.

Again, no answer.

"Fecker!" I shouted, my head bobbing on the second syllable.

"Over here. No need to shout," he said, reclining in his seat down in the lower right of the chamber. The opposite corner of me.

I walked slowly down the aisle toward the front of the chamber, the carpet unable to mute the sound of my feet on the ground. The chandeliers above, both the set of heavy and set of lighter ones, swung on beat with my stepping. Even the gold French curtains of the windows shook. I stopped in the center of the chamber. No one dared to move me.

"It was brought to my attention, earlier this morning, that someone in this chamber has attempted to paint me in a bad light. Not the first time, and most certainly not the last," I said, hands in my pockets still.

There was a soft laughter in the chamber.

"Yes, yes," I started and pulled the newspaper out from under my arm, "no doubt that many of you have seen this. Printed in the paper, from the biggest source *Green Tree News*, was a picture of two individuals entering my home. Now, first off, only Clarkson, the young lad, was a kid. Sixteen. His sister, Theresa, is twenty. They probably didn't remember me, but, secondly, I was good friends with their father."

I stopped, looking around the chamber, holding up the newspaper. Everyone was still.

"What you probably didn't hear about was why they were there. I have made it painfully clear to the entirety of the state, that my home is also my office. You can come knock on my door, and I will answer as quick as I am able," I said and lowered the paper.

"There are certain things I will die on a hill for. Things that I *have* died on a hill for. Things I will let myself get crucified over. And all of you damn well know that! I have been defending the young Governor left and right since she entered office, holding her back from storming down here and cat scratching some of y'all.

"These two had come to me, telling me of their friend Kord. The three of them went exploring in a cave, one they shouldn't have been in, and they admitted to that. Now, you saw the photo. Two entered. Not three, two. That's because the third, Kord, was trapped in the cave."

There was a half-assed gasp that rolled over the chamber.

"Now, from a report form Mayor Smitt of Carlisle, the fiery Puerto Rican who's put us to shame for our inaction, detailed of a hole that would've been big enough for the young man, Kord, to escape. But due to the cave being unmapped, unknown, and from the likelihood of flooding, I cannot allow anyone inside. Legally.

"I have therefore put out an order to the police to conduct a search of the waters and region up and down the Can-not-go-in-it, Conodoguinet. And I will let myself get crucified for demanding that this chamber help in any way they can in the efforts. In addition to calling on Cumberland, Perry, Dauphin, Juniata, and several other surrounding counties into helping directly.

"A lie, however, is not something I will get crucified over, dammit!"

I breathed in deeply and out slowly, scanning the chamber, letting my eyes fall on Fecker. I walked over to him, snapping the paper in front of his face, making sure he could see the image.

"What is this about, Meyer? We're supposed to be commencing a vote," Fecker said.

"Mr. Fecker," I started, looking directly into a camera that broadcasted over PCN, "the only way that they would have gotten this image, from this angle, would be inside your house."

"I thought you said you wouldn't let yourself get crucified over a lie, Meyer."

I turned to him and pointed at the image.

"Mr. Fecker, in the lower righthand corner, one can clearly see the crack from your bedroom window. I know you want to slander me, but to stoop to something like this?" I said, tapping the paper.

"Bull, Meyer. Like always, you're full of yourself," he said, and spat a long, mucus-filled strand of bile over my cheek, neck, and on my sports coat.

I stood straight, still holding the paper close to him in my left hand and turned to face the chamber.

"I rest my case," I said softly.

I launched my right arm forward, through the paper, punching Fecker square in the nose. The blow made a very loud, very distinct crunching noise on impact. Blood squirted from both nostrils and the bridge of his nose as he and his chair fell back onto the floor. He lay there unmoving for a second. The whole of the chamber moved at once, all rustling their clothes, to get a better look.

"Ah, *fuck*!" he screamed in pain, holding his nose.

"Let the record show that he spat on me first, which is assault, and a biohazard to do as well, so I acted in self-defense. Would you all not agree?"

The chamber looked at itself and back to me. A few nodded. Fecker still screamed in pain.

"I will escort myself from the premises now, allowing the president pro tempore to take my spot. Mr. Ronald," I said, motioning to the front of the chamber.

I walked out of the chamber into the hallway, where security was already waiting. I handed them the paper and they talked over what they should do. They asked me how I got to the capital that day. I said by taxi. They then told me that they would drive me first to the police station, then home, where I would be monitored until the case was dealt with fully. I cooperated.

As we walked out of the beautifully designed building and down the steps, the guy with the guitar looked up from his phone, saw me, and smiled. I showed him my handcuffs and shrugged, passing him by. He just smiled and played me a tune, anyways.

When I was put in the back of the security vehicle, a wave of déjà vu rushed over me. But, it was as if it was going to happen, not that it had happened. I shook my head and tried to wash it form my mind.

I leaned back, and exhaustion from weeks of nonstop working hit me like a brick falling off the top of a building. My phone started to ring. Not the one on my belt but the burner phone. The one that couldn't receive calls. And I knew that Theresa and Clarkson couldn't call me. I tried to stay awake, but I was unable to keep the weight of my eyelids up. Just before I fell sleep, in the dark corners of my eyes, closing like irises and shutters around my vision, that crooked smile emerged, that damn, crooked smile.

"Night, night, Meyer. The deed is done," he said.

I fell asleep.

CHAPTER 13

COAL DUST

KORD

Anger is too soft of a word to express how I felt, and rage would suffice if I wanted to admit that I lost my cool. But how couldn't I? For everything that was going on, had gone on, and I assume would continue to happen, there had been no answer as to why. I thought I had just killed a man, all in self-defense mind you, but apparently, I hadn't. A wave of relief ran over me, but I didn't feel closure.

The thing is, I never saw the face of the guy after I came to. If it was truly who I thought it was, then I am disgusted to admit that part of me felt happy. Have him feel what a young me has had to feel for years. I could've done more, made his screams a melody for me to fall asleep to. Use his bones as a xylophone or drum kit to beat and challenge the devil and his cohorts myself. I could've done so much more that…that I don't think he would've deserved. It's funny how life is unfair like that.

"Hey, uh, Kord?" Raef asked over his shoulder.

"What?" I snapped back at him like a dog with its meal in its teeth.

"Jeez, boy, what has you all up in your own ass?"
"Is that even a question I have to answer?"
"Do you want to?"
"Should I?"
"Can you stop answering my question with a question?"
"Perhaps?"
"Kord."
"Maybe if you give me a straight answer for something, I will."

Raef stopped and turned around to face me. He took his flashlight and placed it right on the center of my chest. Having him come toe-to-toe with me, I finally understood at least one thing: Raef was taller, towering. He had a short beard and mustache that connected with his head of hair, which was a medium length and somehow still neatly combed. He could also have trimmed his nose hairs if he even cared to—I doubt he did. His breath smelled like stale mint, not bad but not good. His teeth were all straight. Hair went up the length of his arm and disappeared under his sleeve.

I followed my eyes up that flashlight, and his eyes looked right into mine. They were dark, unwelcoming, shielding something. Looking into those eyes made my heart thud, my brain suspend all thought, and blood ran cold. When he spoke, that accent of his broke the spell.

"I don't know what you're playing at. I don't know why you and your friends decided to even come into this cave in the first place but know just one thing. You will listen to me. You will let me help you out of here. And you will be able to do whatever it is you like to do outside of my domain."

"Your domain?" I asked him.

"Okay, maybe domain is the wrong word. But—"

"Raef, what are you not telling me?"

"What do you mean?"

"What do *I* mean? What in the hell do *you* mean, Raef? Symbols on the walls, going deeper, six chambers with spider webs. Even an eighteenth century Hapsburg, with everything going on in their inbred minds, could figure it out."

Raef tapped his flashlight on my chest. He pursed his lips, eyeing me down and shaking his head. Then he chuckled. He looked up, tapping what had become an extension of his arm at this point, harder against my chest. Each thud shook my rib cage. On the outside I perhaps looked ready, but on the inside, on the inside I was ready to run.

"Don't ask questions, you don't want the answers to."

The chamber shook and some debris fell onto the flashlight. Raef looked down on it, confused. He ran his finger against the steel outside rim of the light. He rubbed his fingers together. I didn't dare move my eyes off of this giant in front of me.

Cocking his head, he shined the light on me. He reached out and brushed off my shoulder something that was dark and dusty. Raef put his hand back under the light.

"Interesting," he said.

"What?"

"Coal dust."

"In Cumberland?"

"It's possible. The whole network isn't fully mapped or studied. It's also possible that we're not in Cumberland County anymore."

"Are there any parts that are fully done? Is there thorium?"

"I mean, for the first part, I guess. For the second, yes, but to get that far, you best give up trying to find a way out at that point. And accept whoever your god is," he said and turned his back to me. "Let's keep moving."

I readjusted my pack and kept walking. And walking. And walking. We never even turned a corner.

* * *

Exhaustion can have many effects on a person. Such as blurry vision, headaches and migraines, poor balance, inability to keep balance, and quick mood changes. Add my dehydration into the mix and you have a recipe for one big problem. I stumbled, fell to my knees, and gasped for breath. Raef, picked me up by my pack, helping me to lean against the cave wall. He took my pack off me, put it in my lap, then handed me my own water bottle. He helped me sip on it, tipping it to my lips and back. Water trickled onto me from the ceiling. I looked up and saw a slim skylight mocking me.

"Let's rest a minute," Raef said, flopping himself against the wall opposite.

"Y-yeah. Let's…do that. Damn," I said and wiped my hand against my forehead, flicking the sweat and coal dust onto the cave floor.

"Keep sipping your water, the darkness itself can play tricks on the mind, and you don't want to give any extra fuel to the fire."

"Ha," I said, sipping my water some more. "I feel like I might've already been hallucinating."

We both nodded, not having to look at each other to know what the other was thinking.

"So, thorium." I said, "That means there is radon, too, isn't there?"

"Yep."

"That's fun."

Silence.

"Tell me about yourself, Raef. Where you from?"

"Huh? Oh…" He looked around, snapping his head up and down the corridor as if being hunted, and he was quiet until he said, "Northern Lebanon."

"Explains the accent. It was the first thing I picked up on. What brought you to America?"

"My parents," he said, in a tone with more to the story he wasn't saying.

"What about them brought you overseas?"

He paused mid sigh and scanned his eyes down both lanes of the corridor. Raef didn't move his head, only his eyes.

"Well, uhhh, I was separated from my parents during the Lebanese Civil War. I was only a kid."

"And they sent you here?"

"No, they uhhh, they left for Egypt, thinking I was dead."

"So why come here?"

"They didn't like America. I didn't like them. That's as much as I'd like to say about it."

The usual metaphor used here is "the silent awkwardness could have been cut with a knife," but I'll spare the trouble of using it. Just know that I hated it. The silence. Any time there was silence was a moment to my thoughts, a moment to hear the ambience, a moment to hear humming. Thankfully, that would be broken by a bit of static from Raef's radio.

"Hello, hello?" a squeaky voice came through the other end. It sounded like an impression of something.

Raef looked around, confused. I pointed to his radio. He grabbed it and looked at it. When the static started again, I swiped it from his hands. Raef didn't protest. I held the button in on the side. It clicked, and the static stopped.

"Hello?" I asked into it. I let go of the button, and the static returned.

"Hello?" it asked back, the static breaking it up. After the "hello" was another voice, but I couldn't tell whose. So, I took a guess and prayed.

"Mr. Conductor? Is that you?"

"You bet your smokestacks it is. We're calling all engines. I repeat! Calling all engines."

"Wow, you're a dork, Clarkson. But man if I ain't glad to hear you."

"It's not just me Kord," Clarkson said.

"'Sup, Kord?" Theresa asked.

"Hot damn! How did you even find me?"

"I noticed a faint signal coming from the mountain and wasn't any frequency channel I recognized. Not even the cops! Speaking of, there's this Martin guy, total asshat—"

"Roll that back, Clarkson," I said.

"How far?" he asked. He actually cranked something.

"What frequency channel is this?" I asked.

"I…I can't tell. All I can tell you is that I was able to home in on it by using a bunch of shit going out my window. Made the whole house an antenna, basically."

"No, you didn't," Theresa spoke loudly from the background.

There was more talking, but something wasn't sitting right. It was great to hear them again, it was like we had been apart for longer than we were. Still, I was unable to focus in on what they were saying. Something wasn't sitting right. I pressed the button.

"Hey, Clarky, how many search parties were sent out?"

There was no answer from them. I could hear them breathing, and I heard Clarkson's lip part as if he were going to say something, but he didn't. There was some shuffling.

"Kord. They were being very weird about it. Very secretive. We had to go to Meyer and personally ask him to do

122 · THE CAVE OF APPALACHIA

something. The only thing that was ever sent out was a dispatch of officers to see if you were still at the cave-in. Other than that, not even Meyer's strong-arming could sway anyone. They kept pointing to the incoming storms," Theresa said.

"What the? But Raef said…"

"Who's Raef?" Theresa asked.

"A search and rescue person…"

"Hey, Kord?" Clarkson asked.

"Yeah?" I talked to the walkie this time, bringing a knee up to my chest, resting my arm on it.

"Where…you…get a radio…talk…s?" Clarkson asked, the signal weakened and filled with static.

I slowly turned my head to where Raef would've been. I looked down the chamber where a shadow now stood, staring right at me. I didn't press the button, but something did click.

CHAPTER 14

A VISIT TO THE GRANDPARENTS

―――

MR. MARTIN

"Mr. Martin, while I do not believe it to be my professional position to ask about your methods as a federal agent, I must ask one question," Ms. Smitt said calmly but with authority.

Clarkson knows that I know what he knows. Confusion is natural to set in during those situations, even frustration. I don't blame the kid, but he has pent up anger inside him that needs to be addressed sooner than later. The thing is, I need him to say what it is so I might be able to help him, his sister Theresa—a sweet young girl, talkative—Kord, and Lord bless us all if I am also able to help this whole world. Meyer is only kept up in his own ambitions.

For now, I needed more on Kord. Ms. Smitt was leading me down a hallway to some room. It wasn't the way to the archives, so I was curious and let her continue.

"That question is what, Ms. Smitt?" I asked, equally as calm.

She grabbed my arm and ducked into a dark unused room. I lost my balance and stumbled into the room, being shoved into a rolling office chair that slammed into a desk. A soft laugh came from a dark corner. Before I had a chance to address it, Ms. Smitt grabbed my shoulders and leaned in close to me.

"What in the *hell* is wrong with you? *What* are you playing at?"

I was taken aback. It had been a good while since I had anyone snap at me like that, and the first time I could remember since…a good while…that it was a woman. I wasn't scared, more so simply surprised.

"What do you mean?" I finally said softly.

"The way you were talking back there."

I slowly moved my hand to her wrists, lightly tapping them from my shoulders. I cocked my head and stood slowly. For as much as I towered over her, she still looked at me with a fire in her eyes like a mother bear.

"Ms. Smitt. There are things going on here that need to be directly addressed for me to do anything. Clarkson will come around to his senses at some point and finally tell me," I said and straightened my blazer. "Now, either that, or Meyer will—"

"That's another thing. Why are you bringing our lieutenant governor into this? Clarkson is a hothead, I'll yield that, but what makes you think he'd know anything about Meyer?"

"Understand this, Ms. Smitt."

"Mayor."

I cleared my throat, hesitating to say more, but I conceded, "Mayor Smitt. I'm here for more than just Kord. I know Meyer. We go back longer than you might think or would accept. I know that bastard like he was my own *biological* brother."

She opened her mouth, not to say something, not to gawk, but she just opened it. She crossed her arms and leaned on one leg. I kept my mouth shut for a bit longer, but she rolled her hand for me to continue. So, I obliged.

"There is a reason for caves in Appalachia being sealed off. They're dangerous for a variety of reasons, and one of them is something you can't, well, won't want to comprehend."

I pulled out my cigarette case, took out a cigarette, packed it, and lit it. The dim glow from the end of my cigarette was the only light in the room, save for the cracks from the doorframe. I took in a deep breath. Then let out a long sigh. I cleared my throat.

"You'd think with how much your people get, you'd do a better job at it," Ms. Smitt said.

I smirked. "I guess they don't pay you to think, do they?"

"They'd have to pay a hell of a lot more, that's for sure."

I began to laugh, but that laughter quickly turned to coughing. I pulled out a handkerchief from my pocket and began coughing into it. What inkling of temptation Ms. Smitt had to laugh along quickly subsided as my coughs became more violent.

"Do you need any—"

"Naw, naw. No. I'll be fine." I said with my coughing slowing. I checked the handkerchief for blood and folded it back up. "Take me to the archives, now. Please, Mayor Smitt."

She turned toward the door, beckoning me to follow. "I'm starting to like when you called me 'Ms. Smitt' more. The way you say mayor is just weird."

I rolled my eyes. "I'll call you whatever you want, just make up your mind at some point."

Each of the record rooms on the first floor smelled of dust and the musk of old, crispy, yellowing paper. Most files were kept on a gliding file track system. Those that weren't kept on the units were stored along shelves on the walls. All the files were kept under locked dust covers in their respective locations, and each room was only accessible by personnel with the appropriate key.

Ms. Smitt was turning the hand crank on the outside of the cabinets, having to put her weight into it to get the old units moving. Upon any offering to help, she shooed me away. The cabinets made a clanking sound each time the internal gears hit a locking notch. The first unit thudded against the wall, kicking up some dust, followed by each unit down.

She started coughing from the dust now floating in the air. I grabbed my blazer's lapel and held it close to my nose and mouth. Thinking it would help, I flipped a fan switch on the wall, only making things worse. Dust flew off the top of the units. Ms. Smitt hit the switch and pulled me out of the room letting the dust settle. Her coughing fit started to fade.

"Do you not have an electronic copy of the files, Mayor Smitt?"

"Kinda. It's like a library. Only certain information is on the computers right now. Thankfully, we know the section they're both in. That said, only so many last names start with C-L-V."

As the rest of the dust settled, we reentered the room. Ms. Smitt took out a pair of keys. She tried a few into the dust cover's lock until one finally turned it. She lifted the cover, propped it up, and, taking a small keyring flashlight, she shined it inside to find the correct manila files. Taking them from the shelf, she handed them to me.

"Here we are. Ms. Mikolis K. Clverson and Mr. Jako S. Clverson. Both from the Ukraine. Both Ruthenian."

"Very good," I said and flipped through them. I then opened my briefcase, slipped them into an elastic pouch, and locked it closed.

"No. No. You're going to hand those back when you're finished looking through them." Ms. Smitt's eyes pierced through me as she crossed her arms.

"On record, the City of Carlisle will get all information at the end of the investigation. This includes city-owned documents. Off the record, you'll see why I need these. Now, Mayor Smitt, if you wouldn't mind as to lock that back up, unless there is anything more you need. I'm done in here for now. I would like to pay a visit to our new Ruthenian friends. You're driving."

She grabbed the cover and lowered it into place, waiting a second to lock it. She eyed me up and down, squinting before locking. I must be saying something wrong to these people to get them so upset at me.

We walked out to Ms. Smitt's black sedan. It made a beep and a sharp click as it unlocked. Clouds started rolling in. I got into the passenger side of the vehicle before Ms. Smitt opened her door. I ducked inside, putting the briefcase between my legs. Ms. Smitt sighed and opened her door and joined me inside. She glanced up to the window for the room where Clarkson and Theresa were, checking if they were still there. Theresa looked back at her through the window, waving. The car started, and we were off.

It started to rain.

* * *

Before long, we pulled up to the house, kicking up dust on the gravel road. Ms. Smitt turned off the sedan and opened the door, putting one foot out and standing up. I bobbed my head around, attempting to look up at the front of the house and around the premises through the front window. She then stepped out.

The land where the house stood had once been farmland and it showed. The topsoil was all stripped away, and the lawn grew more weeds than it did grass; what grass did grow was tarnished in yellowish-brown spots. The edge of a forest was well defined, there was a row of trees that were all almost perfectly aligned—tree roots sprung up out of the ground the closer you got to the edge. The driveway was short and connected to a walkway leading to the front porch. A flowerbed with bushes separated the house and walkway.

"Looks like the rain has either completely missed this place or gone around," I jested.

"So, it seems. Let me do the talking," Ms. Smitt stated, closing her door.

"It's all yours, Mayor Smitt," I said, stepping out of the car and closing the door behind me.

"I plan on it," she said, "The last time two suited people approached either of them, their parents turned up missing."

"How so?" I asked, following Mayor Smitt up the short driveway. The car locked with a honk.

"They're immigrants from the Soviet Union, remember? Your sports jacket would be enough to spook Mr. Clverson probably."

I nodded, half listening, approaching the front porch.

"Understood. Also, it's a blazer."

"The Ukraine," she said, pointing to a small shield with a coat of arms on it, connected to a knocker on the front door.

"Yes, yes. I remember now, Mayor Smitt."

She grabbed the knocker and knocked it three times. We waited for an answer, and when none came, she knocked again. I looked down to my shoes, rocking in them. Mayor Smitt was puzzled, making a bunch of "hmm" and "huh" sounds. She then leaned back to peek through the window. She put her hands up around her face, doing her best to not smudge the glass.

There was a slight movement inside. She turned back to me as I raised my head from my feet. I was expecting her to say something, but she only scrunched up her face in thought. I rolled my shoulders, pecking out my neck, studying our surroundings. She stood there and kept her attention back through the window, then back to me.

"Not home?" I asked.

"Shh," she hissed quite violently and swatted her hand in the air at me. She thought a bit longer.

Again, this woman had me off guard, making my eyes bug out.

"No, they're home," she said and started walking off the porch, "I think they're—"

The door opened, and in the doorway stood a short, older woman using a cane to help hold herself up.

"I'm sorry, I didn't realize that…" She looked directly at Ms. Smitt and a smile grew on her face. The older woman started moving closer to her, "Oh, Willa!"

"Ms. Clverson!" Mayor Smitt said, hugging and kissing her cheeks three times.

"Oh, how nice it is to see you again, deary," Ms. Clverson said.

"Ms. Clverson, this is Mr. Martin," Ms. Smitt said, motioning to me.

I reached out my right hand to her. I gave her a soft smile and bowed my head. She grabbed my hand and shook it, giving me a warm smile back.

"You two, come in. Come in please," Ms. Clverson said and motioned for them to enter. "Would you care for some water or coffee?"

"Oh, no. Thank you, Ms. Clverson. We just have some questions for you is all. I pray we didn't interrupt anything," I said.

"Who's there? Whose voice?" A voice bellowed from an opening for a den down the hall.

"It's Willa and a cohort of hers," Ms. Clverson said.

There was an annoying squeaking sound followed by a clicking. An elderly man walked out from the den. He walked slowly, and his face showed his experienced years, but his posture was no different from a young adult. His hair was a light gray and combed back. Individual strands rested in front of his ears. He wore a beige button-up shirt tucked into a pair of brown trousers.

He took a few more steps down the hall. Pulling a pair of glasses from his shirt pocket, he put them on and flickered his eyes. He took another step and halted. He swallowed and smacked his lips. A color-filled face drained and went almost white.

"Sir, are you okay? I hope my appearance isn't too formal." I cocked my head and tried to appear like an innocent puppy. When that didn't work, I looked toward Ms. Clverson and Mayor Smitt, asking, "Is he okay?"

"Mr. Clverson," Ms. Smitt waved her hand to Mr. Clverson, "it's all alright, Mr. Clverson. It's me, Willa."

The old man reached into his back pocket and dabbed his forehead with a handkerchief, removing his glasses. He turned around and started back toward the den, motioning for us to follow. "Would you like some wooter while I'm up?"

"Go ahead and fill a pitcher, darling," Ms. Clverson said, closing the door behind us. She tugged on Mayor Smitt's arm, pulling her further into the house.

I tipped myself up on my toes and allowed myself to fall back down on my heals. I pursed my lips and mumbled, "Guess we're having wooter."

Ms. Clverson turned off the TV and sat down on an olive-colored conversational couch. She beckoned for Mayor Smitt and me to join her. Mayor Smitt took a seat next to Ms. Clverson. She rested comfortably and slid into the couch, crossing her legs at the knee. I sat on the edge of the cushion, leaning on an arm rest, away from the two. I pulled out my notepad and pen and started to open the other side of my blazer. I stopped, feeling the sharp glare Ms. Smitt was giving me. I didn't even bother asking, so I just patted that side closed.

Mr. Clverson returned with a pitcher of water and put it on a small coffee table with four glasses. He poured each one half full, except for his own, which was nearly full to the brim. He took a long sip and sat down in a wooden rocker. He took a deep breath, closed his eyes, and leaned back in the rocker. It clicked and squeaked with each rock. He then put his head up straight, and opened his eyes, looking directly at me.

I looked at Mr. Clverson, and then darted my eyes around. They reset back upon the Ruthenian's gaze. I reached for my pocket, and Mr. Clverson froze, his eyes going wide. I slowly pulled out a pocket watch, clicked it open, and wrote the time down on my pad. I then put the watch away. Mr. Clverson still stared at me with a solid defense behind his eyes. The only thing I was able to read about him was his fear over my appearance but nothing else.

"Is something the matter, Mr. Clverson?" I turned to Ms. Clverson, "Have I offended him on accident?"

"Mr. Martin, it's not that," Ms. Clverson started.

"You look very official and yet not at the same time," Mr. Clverson said.

"Mr. Clverson, rest assured, I mean no harm at all. I am here to ask questions yes, but I hope not to raise any suspicion that there's anything else than that. I do not speak Russian. I can't even speak my native language that well, let alone English. Again, I do not mean to alarm you by our presence, but we merely have some questions about Kord."

"Where are you from, Mr...." Mr. Clverson leaned forward in his chair. Waiting for him to say more, I realized that he was instead waiting on me.

"Oh! Martin. Mr. Martin. Paulsboro, New Jersey. I'm with the National Park Service."

I kept my voice as level as possible.

"New Jersey, huh?"

"Yes. Mr. Clverson, I—"

"I remember the court case between New Jersey and New York of Ellis Island. I had nothing else better to do than keep up with that. It's funny, ya know, states fighting over an island."

"Remember last year, the *Pennsylvania v. Ohio v. New York* case over a stretch of islands in Lake Erie?"

"Yes, yes, and then it was brought before the court that the islands were actually Canadian."

Ms. Smitt leaned toward Ms. Clverson, "What are they talking about?"

Ms. Clverson leaned back. "Haven't a clue."

I chuckled and said, "I have to hand it to you, Mr. Clverson, your English is quite good."

"I've been in this country longer than you have, Mr. Martin. I'd dare say, my English is better than yours."

I smiled and held back correcting him. "That it is, that it is." I picked up my glass of water. Pointed its brim toward Mr. Clverson and took a sip.

"I hate to break up the fun, but Mr. Martin and I are here for an important reason. It is in regard to your grandson, Kord," Ms. Smitt said.

There was a brief, echoed silence in the room that was broken by Ms. Clverson clearing her throat. She lowered her head, curling in her lips. Her mouth opened but nothing came out.

"Is he okay? Do you have anything more you know about where he is? How he's doing?" Mr. Clverson spoke for her.

"We are unsure, Mr. Clverson," I spoke before Mayor Smitt could. "His last confirmed location was along the Conodoguinet Creek. His kayak was anchored and tied off to a landing. Moreover, he was with his friends." I looked to Mayor Smitt. "And I'm sure you've already been briefed on that," I said, retreating back in my seat.

Mr. Clverson narrowed his eyes and stopped rocking his chair. It came to a slow halt. He stood up, taking his glass with him. "If there were anyone for him to get lost with, those two were probably the ones he'd do it with. And there wouldn't be anyone else I'd trust if it happened. They are practically Kord's siblings."

He walked to a sliding door and stepped out on the deck, closing the door behind him. I exchanged a concerned expression with Ms. Smitt. I started to get up to follow him.

"Don't. It's best to leave him alone when he goes out on the porch like that," Ms. Clverson said.

I sat back down.

"Do you know…" she stopped, looking us over. "What do you need to know?"

Mayor Smitt spoke, "Well, is there anything about Kord that could potentially shorten our time frame for finding him? Anything that I wouldn't already know. Allergies, to start with."

Ms. Clverson picked up her water. She took a small sip. Sighed. Then threw back the rest of the nearly full glass like a shot. There was something about it that I understood, but I didn't know why or how I felt it.

"Ms. Clverson. Miko," Mayor Smitt said putting her hand on Ms. Clverson's knee.

"Kord has a severe case of anxiety," she said, "We think it was brought on by a past incident. It used to be so bad that he would hallucinate. He was very young, so we always thought it was his imagination. It got to a point where he would cry at night. Some of the things he said he'd see did scare us, like claiming to see a man in the corner, so we took him to a psychologist and then to a priest to bless him. We also tried just to get him to talk. Umm…" She thought for a second.

I repositioned myself in my chair. I nodded my head and tapped my fingers together.

"Why is Kord in your custody?" I asked. "Did something happen to the father or mother?"

"We never knew who the father was. The mother was our own daughter, Ewa. She was a happy person, wasn't the most financially stable, but she managed with long working hours. Sometimes she would have to take Kord to work with her when we weren't home. We were in Ontario at the time, visiting an old friend of ours, David Penelope. He was a draft dodger during Vietnam. Anyways, we were visiting when we got a call that Ewa was in a car accident. She had Kord with her. Kord made the call. Kord had a broken wrist. The other driver had fled the scene but was caught later with just a concussion. Ewa…Ewa didn't make it.

"The paramedics said that the impact would've been enough to…well, yeah. But in reality, it wasn't just the impact that got her. The car had crumpled and stabbed into her. Kord saw the whole thing. He always said that there was another person in the car with them, but he didn't know who they were, and there was really no way to tell if there truly was."

"I…I never knew that that was Ewa," Ms. Smitt said. "I never made the connection. We've been friends for so long, and you didn't tell me?"

"I didn't want to tell you, and I didn't want you to know, darling," Ms. Clverson said.

"Why, Miko?" Ms. Smitt asked.

Ms. Clverson didn't answer. No one spoke for about a minute, the only sound coming from a ticking clock.

"Okay, so let's make sure we keep this straight, Ms. Clverson," I began. "Kord suffers from a severe case of anxiety possibly brought on by Post Traumatic Stress Disorder. Do you think that there might be a connection between him claiming to see someone in the accident and then seeing someone in his room?"

"I don't think there'd be a direct connection, if any," Ms. Clverson said.

"And why is that?"

"It was only in his room he would see it. He was fine getting in and out of cars after the accident. It also only started when we moved into this house. Then it got tested for radon, which we had a fair bit of."

"Radon can't cause hallucinations, I thought," Ms. Smitt said.

"You're correct, Mayor Smitt, but radon has been shown to have an effect on people who already suffer from illnesses that might cause hallucinations or visions," I chimed in.

"He's correct, Willa," Ms. Clverson said, "However, they seemed to stop after a while. We had the house treated for the radon, and he eventually stopped having the hallucinations. Every now and again, the actual heightened anxiety will rear its head, but is usually a short spell of maybe five minutes. Other than that, the only other thing I can think of is that he usually doesn't sleep the whole way through the night, and instead will wake up from time to time."

A grandfather clock from somewhere else in the house spoke up, alerting us of the late afternoon. I finished writing down some notes and checked my watch. I put the notepad and pen back in my blazer, tapped Mayor Smitt's shoulder, and nodded to Ms. Clverson. When I stood up and stretched, all my joints popped and cracked. The other two stood up after me.

"Ms. Clverson, I would like to thank you for your and your husband's time. I think I have gathered all I will need.

However, if we have anything else to speak about with you, may we come back here?"

"I'd actually rather you didn't come here. However, we will gladly make the trip to Willa's office."

"Very well."

"If there is anything more you need to tell us later on, please give my mobile a ring, Miko," Mayor Smitt said and grabbed Ms. Clverson's hand.

"Of course, deary." She hugged Mayor Smitt.

Ms. Clverson saw us to the door and waved us off, closing the door with a slight aggressiveness. When the car unlocked, it made a beep and soft click. I stepped inside, putting the briefcase between my legs and closed the door.

* * *

On the car ride back, I looked out the window, lost deep in thought biting my thumbnail.

"Oy, Mr. Martin. Down there is the intersection it happened at, the crash," Ms. Smitt said, pointing at the street signs.

"Pull over then, I just want to check it out."

Ms. Smitt pulled over and let the car idle. I stepped out, and she followed me.

"Careful where you step, Martin. There's still glass that gets swept up from time to time. Let alone stepping in a pothole and twisting your ankle."

I leaned against the car, my door still open. "I couldn't even imagine what would go through a little kid's mind witnessing what happened. I think I understand why Clarkson was the way he was earlier. I owe him an apology, Ms. Smitt."

"It would be best to make it an opening comment and then just let it go."

"Yeah, I agree. But I still need him to open up and tell me what I need to know. Something tells me that he knows more about Kord than Theresa does."

Studying the surroundings, my eyes landed on a figure standing out in the field. It was tall, not completely dark, but it was in shadow. I knew who it was, and seeing him, I knew what to do.

I grabbed my briefcase and propped it up in my seat. I unlocked it. It opened with two distinct clicks. I paused for a second, shuffling through everything.

"Huh."

"What's wrong, Mr. Martin. Everything there?"

"Yeah, everything is here. You did lock the car, didn't you?"

"I did, why?"

"I thought I heard you lock it. Let me show you why I needed them." I beckoned for her to come over.

"Mr. Martin, what's wrong?"

"When I put Mr. and Ms. Clverson's documents in here, it was just like that. Mr. Clverson was on top."

"And?"

"Now Ms. Clverson is on top," I said and looked to Mayor Smitt.

CHAPTER 15

LIEUTENANT GOVERNOR CHINKWE MEYER IS AN OLD FRIEND OF MINE

?

Meyer leaned over a sink and coughed. He coughed. He hacked. He bled from the mouth. Meyer looked into the mirror at a reflection that resembled himself, but he knew it was really me looking back. I smirked at him as his expression turned ever more sour toward me.

"Lieutenant Governor Chinkwe Meyer was an old friend of mine, but now he uses an alias. I've known him ever since the time I was sealed into my wood home. But he knew I would not be kept buried. He was not the only one. There were more. But he is more of a link than the others. While I have been able to keep my name, keep my skin, they choose to allow themselves to change and be born again. But Meyer, that easily swayed fool, can be captured with the single appearance of what was given as a protector but is now made to be a symbol of death and evil. He of all people should surely know, right? And yet he lets the ever-changing world change him. I, on the other hand, have caused the change in the world. So, if one were to think about it, Meyer changes when I tell him to. He is my clay, and I am his sculptor. Such pity that fool made of clay has power.

"Meyer had come to me when I was still ensnared in the quagmire that he, Martin, and the others set for me. Yet still, I was of help to Meyer when he so asked. And he has the gall to say that Martin has a silver tongue. Ha!"

"Damn you. Shut up," Meyer growled at me. It was a low growl, a guttural growl.

"Ha ha. Meyer asked me for the type of help that only a man tired in faith, trust, and emotion has. If he could have power, then he wanted to have it. He lusted for it. And so, he got the power he desired. Because I made it so.

"He had come to me on a night that someone would go to the devil for an extra hand. I pulled strings for him through the acts of others. I could cause pain, troubles, and return the world to chaos, and Meyer would accept it and do nothing while Martin would look into a shadowed corner, yell, and make a scene. Martin would get people's attention and fight the darkness."

"Shut. Up." Meyer pounded his fist on the ledge of his sink.

"Martin would rather flail about in the dark and kill himself through his lungs just to have some light around him. But Meyer wanted to use me and keep me alone. He would take steps that others despised. Only a few who stepped upon the podium I gave them would make it. And yet, so many peoples and persons tried. The masses loved them at first, and then they saw what those groups did. They revolted against it. And what did Meyer, the ever so loved quiet giant do? Meyer accepted it.

"Did Meyer use me to become a Caesar? I know he did. Did he know that alone he could not hurt me? I know he thought he could, but he really could not. Was he thankful? Can a man who wants the death of me, be thankful for granting a wish? To help fulfill his lust? No, he cannot," I told him.

"Oy! Shut up. You are going to stay there, and you're not coming out," Meyer huffed and then hacked again.

I cackled and said, "They will come for you, Meyer. They are on their way. My brothers. They will come for you and you cannot stop that."

"I said shut it, you bastard. I do my end of the deal, you do yours, and then you leave me alone, got it?"

"Ha, ha, ha. Oh, Meyer. It's been too long for you, hasn't it?"

The mirror shattered into a fine dust and mist with shards falling into the sink and poking through his fingers. The bleeding coming from his hand now matched the blood in color and smell that was hocked up from his stolen lungs. The lights of his bathroom lit the room entirely, but still it let itself fall into the shadows. I smiled at Meyer. My mouth and eyes now made only many times more visible in the sink, on the original mirror, and now through his hand. In every possible shard that I looked at him, he looked back.

"The drunkard had already died. For good. The other one will judge too quickly. I may now have two names, but these are not the names they can't be," Meyer said, sighing, and sitting on the edge of the tub.

"Pity, the Catholics only had to be armed with a cross at the front of the Roman lines. Ours has to feel the pain of eternal damnation," I said.

"No," Meyer was quick to snap, "he chose his path. He was willing to take bare what we couldn't."

"What do you call walking this earth for all time? It is what I have to do, and I will tell you it's damnation."

"Go screw yourself. Granted, I guess we already did that ta' you back home, in Levant and North Africa."

"Aye. I have seen the fate of the drunkard already. He was in here, in the cave with us, and our boy Kord put him out of his misery."

"Or so you made him think."

Meyer plucked the shards of glass from his fist; each one being pulled out only bringing more blood with it. He got up and walked to the sink. Meyer washed his hand, opened a cabinet over the toilet, and he pulled out a roll of medical tape which he wrapped around his fingers. He breathed in deeply and out slowly, keeping his eyes closed. Even then I could look back at him.

"Time's ticking, Meyer," I said while his eyes were still closed.

He opened his eyes. He closed the cabinet. He looked at me in the mirror.

"Tick, tock. Tick, tock," I mocked him.

I held a small marionette in front of my chest, swinging it to and fro.

"I have a phone call to make. You do nothing," he said, pointing his wrapped-up hand at me.

I cackled again and said, "The poor forgotten drunkard is with me, Meyer. It's almost your time to join."

"Not while this Kord kid is still stuck with you. Soon it will be time for you to join Martin and me in death."

He left the bathroom, lights still on, floor still a mess, dust and shards still in the sink. The shadows of the room still of my domain.

CHAPTER 16

SNEAKING IS BETTER THAN RUSHING

THERESA

The pattering of the rain on the window could've been thunder itself to my ears. I didn't know if it was Tropical Storm Danielle or Earl rolling over, but it didn't matter at that particular moment. Clarkson, my little rat of a brother, was hanging his head back over the chair—breathing heavily, trying to calm himself. If ever I could read minds, now would've been the best time to know how. Just to know the pain he was feeling as well as I. Then again, it's probably best that I can't.

The window started to feel cool against my back, making the sweat running down feel…wrong. I slid off the windowsill; more like just standing up since my feet already reached the ground. Was Kord having more fun than us right now? I don't know. Knowing him though, he was probably doing just fine. He had his Walkman and spare batteries for all his gadgets. He was prepared for almost anything, but how prepared can you really be? Kord must be okay. He had to be.

"Ohhhhhh," Clarkson started, as if singing.

"What?" I asked him.

"I wish I was in the land of traitors, rattle snakes, and alligators!"

"Okay, I'll bite. What does that have to do with anything?"

"It doesn't. Just letting out...something," he said, jumping up from the chair.

"What's with the sudden burst of energy?"

"Don't know. Gotta do something. What we going to do, huh? Any ideas? Something, something, something," he chatted, marching around in a circle.

"Clarkson."

He stopped and looked at me like an intrigued elementary school student.

"Are you okay?" I asked him.

"Yeah," he snapped quickly, rubbing his hands, "yeah. Yeah, I-I-I will be."

"Clar—"

"I'mma get that bitch back. 'Is that what you tell the ladies?'" he mumbled.

"Clarkson. Stop it. Getting upset is not going to get anything done."

"Yeah well... You're not wrong. I just don't want to admit I am," he said, relaxing his hands.

Before I could say anything else, there was a vibration on my hip. I snapped my head down to it, getting startled by just how violent the so-called "silent mode" on the burner could be. I moved my shirt aside, grabbed the leather holster, fiddled with it, tried to get the damn thing to open so I could grab the phone. It had already rung twice when I finally got it off. I held it in my hand, letting it buzz the two more times before it declined the call. Third buzz came. Waited the four seconds to the fourth buzz. It came, and the phone gave a double buzz indicating the call wasn't answered. As per instruction, we waited.

Time passed, counting the seconds go by in long strides. Nothing came.

"What ya think that—" Clarkson started before the phone rang again, shutting him up.

I answered.

"I almost forgot my own instructions I gave the both of you," came the Philly-heavy accented Lieutenant Governor Meyer.

"We were beginning to wonder who actually called us," I teased back.

"Wait, did someone else call you?" he asked.

"Oh, no. No. See, you just took a while to come through on our end again."

"Oh…" he said, leaving that awkward silence that came when we first talked with him.

I waited for him to say something, and I guess he waited for the same. Clarkson looked at me, flipping his palms upward and spreading out his fingers. There was what sounded like someone sweeping glass on Meyer's end.

"So, uh, oh—" I and Meyer said in unison.

Again, silence. Clarkson rolled his eyes and put his hand out again for the phone. I put up a finger, waiting to see if anything would be said, but nothing came through. I put the phone in Clarkson's hand. He promptly put it to his ear.

"Mr. Meyer. It's Clarkson," he said, nodding his head on his own name.

"Hey, Clarkson." I could hear Meyer's voice through the speaker.

Clarkson recoiled his head and turned down the volume.

"Hey. Listen, we just got done speaking with Ms. Smitt and a certain Mr. Martin."

Clarkson's eyes drooped and he looked at me annoyed, miming like he was smoking a cigarette.

"Yeah. He was kinda an asshat. Got in my fac— No. I wasn't scar— Yes, I gave him some attitude bac— Where'd he go? Oh, I don't know," Clarkson said, rolling his eyes and putting his free hand on his head.

"Probably Kord's grandparents' house. They turned that way on East North Street," I said.

"You mean North East Street? We're not on East North Street," Clarkson said.

"Well yeah, but I can see North East from the window here."

"So, they got out onto East North and then took North East. Which way on North East?"

"West. Remember that Wolf's Bridge is still closed on Wolf's Bridge Road, so you gotta take Route Eleven to Spring Road for West Middlesex."

"Gotcha," Clarkson told me, giving a thumbs up and turned back to the phone, "Meyer, ya there? They got out onto East North and then to North East heading west. Don— Don— Don't worry. It's his grandparents' house. That's where we think they're headin— Meyer! It's the only idea we got."

There was an uncomfortable silence after that snap.

"Yes, yes. Okay. Brown briefcase. Beat up. Find out what he has. Put it back exactly. Gotcha. Yes. Yes. We will be careful. Alright. Okay."

Clarkson kept up the same response for a hot second—repeating 'okay' for a minute or so—until he finally hung up the phone. He pinched his temple and handed the phone to me.

"You couldn't have just told him 'the grandparents'?" I asked, taking the phone.

"Yeah, yeah. What's on second and I dunno who's on third. Let's go before he calls back," Clarkson said with a deep sigh.

* * *

I pulled off to the side of the road, just before the road dipped down for a barely used train trestle to go overhead. Not too far from the bridge was the gravel road for the Clversons' home. When we got out of the car, we made our way to sneak up on the house. We were thankful to not have any cars pass by while we snuck, slinked, and slithered our way into the small forest around their house. About half a mile off of the property, from our current sanctity of an inkberry bush, we looked out upon the vast open land that led up to the back of the house.

I held Clarkson back as Mrs. Clverson came into view of their kitchen window. She looked out of the window, lowering her shoulders, and returned after a bit. Clarkson looked to me, and I to him, then we snuck out from our bush. Keeping low, we rounded our way around the edge of the small forest. We came upon the side of the house and, there it was, in the driveway, the black sedan—Ms. Smitt's black sedan. I started toward it, motioning for Clarkson to stay in the brush.

The rolling bearings of the back sliding door sounded, alerting us that someone was leaving the house. It rolled back, making a thud as it bounced back and closed completely. Our world halted like a valedictorian's who misses one bonus point. Grunting from what was unmistakably Mr. Clverson whipped us back to reality. I continued on sneaking to the car.

If I know Ms. Smitt, then... I thought as the car door popped right open. Just as Clarkson told me again in the drive over here, there was a brown briefcase. Peeking my head through the window of the open car door, I placed the briefcase onto the passenger seat—opening it as I did. In it was two large files and some smaller papers. I took Mr. Clverson's file and flipped through its papers. *Nothing of importance* I assumed. I did it again with Mrs. Clverson's. Same thing. I was stumped. I then looked through all of the other papers in the solid biz-pouch. Nothing. I looked to Clarkson, shaking my head, and popping up my shoulders.

The front door then squeaked. Without thinking, I put the files back in the case and closed it, setting it carefully back on the floor of the car. Ms. Smitt blocked the doorway, looking at Mrs. Clverson. The eyes from a towering Mr. Martin were bright like headlights compared to the rest of his shaded face. I closed the car door gently, making sure it latched. Mr. Martin kept most of his focus on Mrs. Clverson and Ms. Smitt, but when I went to close the car door, they darted toward me—feeling like they were piercing the car's body—and I barely got under the car in time. He shrugged, rocked his head, and turned his attention back to the women still talking.

I rolled out on the opposite side of the car, just out of view of the door. I swung myself behind a tree, peeping out from behind it at Clarkson on the opposite side of the forest. Mr. Martin and Ms. Smith finally got into the car after an eternity. The gravel rustled underneath the car's wheels, silencing as they continued off to the main road.

The bearings of the back screen door opened and closed. Mr. and Mrs. Clverson started talking to one another. I booked it for the forest's edge where Clarkson was, diving behind a tree opposite of him, both our backs to the trees, to the house. I was out of breath.

"Hey, sis, anything?"

I shook my head, still breathing heavily, patting the tree softly. Clarkson waited for me to speak.

"N-no. Just the, *huff*, the city records about Kord's grandparents. Some pens, *huff*, and a pack of cigarettes. Nothing out of the ordinary, I think," I said.

"Huh…" He paused. "Did you put everything back as it was?"

"Yes, uh, yeah," I said, eyes wide toward the ground.

"You sure?"

I shook my head, my eyes pleading for him to forgive me. He rolled his head slowly, sighing.

"Clark—"

He brought his hand up flat, his mouth tight, and I stopped speaking. He uttered one simple word, "Shit."

CHAPTER 17

APOPHENIA

CLARKSON

It felt like it was late into the evening. The rain pounded outside, coming down in sheets, letting up every couple of minutes into a brief moment of pattering. It was dark, hard to see outside, and the sky was a vast array of gray clouds and deep blue that reminded me of the Allegheny Mountains. The microform made a clicking sound as I scanned through it, making a soft static as it did. I was tired, felt like going to bed, it was only sixteen hundred, four in the afternoon. I was tired, so tired.

I was listening into the radio, not hearing anything but static for the past few days since we went to see Meyer. At one point, there was a faint signal coming from the mountains, but nothing strong enough to connect to. The fuzzy static buzzed against my ears, just like the rain outside. I fruitlessly fiddled with the different knobs, sliders, and switches on the equipment.

Dad taught me how to build this contraption, and I am able to keep it functioning, but how it exactly functions, I don't know. Dad had an odd obsession into keeping secrets from the Feds. More than I admit that I do. He never had a problem it seemed with the State. Then again, apparently, he and Meyer knew each other. Something that I never knew of. So be it.

I took the headphones off and listened to the patter of rain against the roof, leaning back in my chair. I tapped my finger against my leg, mimicking my heartbeat. I closed my eyes and began to drift off to sleep.

An all too familiar *thud thud thud thud* against the hardwood in the hallway helped in making me nod off. Then it meowed. And it was a long, loud, and high-pitched meow. The thudding turned into soft pats against my carpet, the meowing growing closer. I opened my door to find the cat giving me a guilty stare from almost clawing the doorframe. It slowly lowered itself onto the ground and sat, staring at me.

I reached down my hand and it instantly sprung up and forward to rub its fluffy little head against my hand, purring all the while. I smiled, letting it do its thing, then tousled its fur before retreating my hand. It lay down in the doorframe, purring, kneading the carpet.

I turned back to my equipment and scanned my eyes down the rows of lights, knobs, et cetera. Nothing came to mind. I sighed, letting the chair fall back onto all fours. I picked up my notepad and reviewed the notes I had taken up to the point of no signal. There were only two things that still stuck out to me: the "Code Appalachia," and when the machine spoke "Meyer" in broken frequencies.

"Code Appalachia": eighteen, thirteen. Naught. Fourteen, nine, twenty. Naught, nil. Eighteen, one, thirteen.

"That's still a dumb as hell name," I muttered to myself.

I picked up a pen sitting in a little metallic *Day of the Dead* themed cup that my oldest sis made for my birthday a year or so ago. Bub of course was front and center on the cup, always facing me, but his glare off into the distance.

I rolled my fingers against the small desk where all the equipment sat, thinking. Naught was said twice, thirteen was said twice and eighteen was said twice. Naught means zero, or nothing, and so does Nil in tennis. The topmost number was twenty. With no other idea in mind, I jot down each number's letter equivalent.

One was A. Nine was I. Thirteen was M. Fourteen was N. Eighteen was R. Twenty was T. And naught/nil I used as spaces. When I finished translating it, it said "RM NIT RAM."

Oh great, Latin, I thought. I tossed down the pen and picked up the pad. I tapped it against the desk end. *Naught-Nil.*

"What do you think, Bub?" I asked allowed, looking to the cup. The cat also let out a small noise.

His dead gaze, his focus, grabbed by the machinery it always seemed.

"Naught-nil. Zero-zero. Nothing-nothing. No-no," I muttered to myself, "Double negative."

I rewrote "NIT RAM" as "NITRAM." I rolled my fingers against my desk.

The cat meowed and I nearly rocked out of my seat to find Theresa looming over me through the doorframe. I threw the pad back onto the desk, holding my hand to my chest, squeezing it.

"Jesus, sis," I said through my gritted teeth.

"What ya up to?" she asked, tilting her head to read the pad. "RM NITRAM?"

"If ya must know, you little shit."

"You're shorter than me, Clark."

"Yeah-ya. Anyways, I haven't been able to get any signal over this thing for the past couple days, so I'm just looking over this to try and find any information in it," I said, tapping the pad.

"Well…" she said and licked her lips, looking at the ceiling, "Nitram… Charcoal, like those art pens. Nitra, the Slovakian city, or the Latin phrase *Nitram rebma*, which I think is purest beauty or something like that."

She rolled her head back down, looking at me. I rubbed my chin.

"What do you think RM could mean?" I asked her.

She tilted her head once more, shook it, shrugged, and sighed before saying, "I don't know. In *StarCraft* it meant remake, but in Linux it means remove."

I crossed my legs at the knee, leaned forward, keeping my attention at the pad for the most part. Theresa leaned against the doorframe, her arms crossed, drumming her fingers on her upper arm.

The cat got up and waddled out of the room. Theresa and I watched as it stopped in the hallway. It licked itself, lifting a hind leg, fully exposed. It suddenly stopped and snapped its head down the hallway, then took off. I rolled my eyes. Theresa was about to say something when the cat hissed loudly. Theresa and I exchanged looks, and she went to go check on it.

The thunder rolled, hammering us from the sky. I paid little attention and turned back to the pad with Theresa now gone. What Theresa said stuck in my mind, about removing or remaking beauty or charcoal. It was abstract, and I still had no idea what it meant.

I rolled my neck and stretched. A chill went through me, my hairs stood on end, and it felt like something tapped my shoulder. Twisting in my chair, I found nothing behind me that wasn't there before. I turned my head back to my room, and nothing was there.

"Uh-huh. Was that you, Bub?" I joked.

Bub didn't say anything, but I could imagine him making some type of sound. The poor guy, he had remembered humanity, and he was left alone in the caves wandering around alone, not like anything else around him. Did he revert to being a creature? At least he wouldn't have been alone, but it would be sad to say the least. He had learned to communicate, basic communication mind you, but communicate, nonetheless.

"Got anything, Bud? Bubby, Bubbo," I joked again.

Again, of course, he said nothing. Verbally. But maybe he was saying something to me. I followed his eyesight to the wall behind the chair, opposite the equipment. We had covered it in a sheet of cork that was just thick enough for a push pin to go through and not pierce the drywall. On the cork, in Bub's eyesight, was the letter Dad had left for me.

I fluttered my eyes then looked back to Bub. His dead gaze no longer seemed to be mindless, but focused. I swore he smiled at me. Taking the letter from the cork, I unfolded the paper. I had a feeling that mine was unlike Theresa's or my oldest sister's. The only uncryptic thing written was "I love you." This followed:

1. Baker Street. Chorus.
2. Kay. Impressed.
3. Legends and Connections
4. Patterns.

And that was it. I pursed my lips and whistled, trying to make sense of it. I sighed, defeated. I got up from my chair and paced around in my room, tapping the pen off of my lips, the letter held behind my back.

"What ya doing?" Theresa asked, watching me from the hallway, carrying the cat.

"Thinking. What was it hissing at?" I asked her, still pacing.

"Nothing, his own shadow I guess," she said, petting him.

It was purring, but then it stopped again—suddenly. It squirmed violently in Theresa's arms until it finally rolled out. It dashed down the hall. To a dark corner and hissed into it. Theresa and I exchanged our confusion.

We had less than a second to do so, however. The radio, having been static for so long, started squealing and wailing like a child throwing a temper tantrum.

SH-E-R-M-A-A-A-N. It yelled at us in broken frequencies. Theresa held her ears and fell to her knees, breathing quick and shallow. She kept rolling her tongue, making a sound that ended with an F, like a woof. I stood there, in a trance.

Theresa made a whimpering sound that took me out of the trance, and I ran to switch off the radio, tripping over some of the books I had piled on the floor from organizing my shelves. I flipped the master control, but it didn't power down. I flipped every switch I could, power or not, and nothing was happening. During this frantic switching, I knocked the cup from the desk. It bounced on the floor and rolled a bit, the contents, mostly pens, spilling out. The metallic clinging it made caught my attention. Bub's gaze was pointing toward the back of the desk, underneath it. I shot my eyes around in their sockets, trying to think of what to do.

Then it hit me. I dropped to my knees and unplugged the master control from the outlet. With no way to get power to it, I thought it would power down. I began to panic when the radio only got louder, but then it did wind down.

I got up and stammered back over to Theresa, taking care over the books. I held her, trying to get her to say something other than what she was muttering. Her breathing slowly became calmer.

"It's okay, sis. It's okay. It's off," I said, carefully putting my hands on hers.

I pulled her hands away from her ears, marks from where she dug in her nails shined red; one mark bled a little. She was trembling, stifling back tears, eyes still clenched tight. She still mumbled something.

"Theresa."

No answer.

"Theresa," I said, softly smacking her cheek.

She stopped muttering and opened her eyes.

"I didn't expect it to be that loud. Let alone to make you hold your ears like that," I said.

"Who is that?" she asked.

"Who was what?" I asked, looking around.

"What?"

"What do you mean what?" I asked her, looking back at her.

"You asked 'who was what.'"

"Because you asked."

"When?"

"Just a second ago."

Her eyes were open, she was genuinely confused, and then she held her head. "Ooow."

"What's wrong, sis?"

"Headache."

I sighed and helped her to her feet, saying, "Let's get you downstairs."

As we went downstairs, I watched the cat thud around like nothing happened, going into my room, stepping over books, and then it jumped up onto my bed.

When we got downstairs, I helped Theresa sit down in her spot on the recliner. I walked past our mom on the couch, into the small kitchen that felt straight out of the fifties. I set a glass in the sink and turned on the faucet. Her glass filled up while I got her some pain killers. I carried them back to Theresa who accepted. Static still rang in my ears and felt like it was getting louder.

"What happened to the radio?" Mom asked.

"Dunno, must've been loud enough to really hurt Theresa's ears, though," I said.

"You okay?" Mom asked, turning to Theresa.

Theresa nodded, mumbling, "I will be."

I leaned against the wall, looking at the TV.

"What you watching?" I asked.

"Nothing really. Nothing good is on," Mom said.

"Gotcha."

She flipped through the channels, stopping for a second at each one to see what was on, but most of the channels were just static, strange since usually it gave a message. Antenna must have been busted. I looked over my shoulder to see the first break in the rain in a while. I watched the rain drain from the busted downspout, streaming down the kitchen window above the sink. I walked over and pressed my face into the glass, looking up into the sky. It was still dark, but beams of sunlight poked through. I leaned off the glass and rocked on my feet.

The static grew louder. I turned back toward Mom and Theresa. I was about to say something, but my voice and all the air from my lungs was stolen from me. I never heard her come in, nor knew she would be back. At the front door, which was next to the stairs, was my oldest sister.

The rain started up heavy again outside. There was static, only static. Static in my ears, static through my arms and legs, static in my mind, and my sight slowly turning to static. I was frozen in place. She couldn't be here. Not physically. I squeezed the sides of the counter tighter and tighter but was squished like clay and faded into static in my grasp. My eyes watered. I blinked.

And she was towering over me. Her face was like looking into a discounted cable channel. Her eyes were black like pits with a small white dot in the center. Her mouth was agape, screeching a static noise at me. It, too, was an abyss. I was being swallowed by this abyss, and at the bottom was a man looking up at me. He had a large, hooked nose, and he was crying, trying to crawl up an invisible rock side, but kept slipping down.

I tried to swing my arms to push her away from me, but I couldn't move them. It was like I had no feeling and that she was holding them down at the same time. My sheer existence felt under siege, like Orléans, and I wanted to give up, surrender.

"Clarkson," a soft and raspy voice said. Whoever it was grabbed my shoulder.

"Clarkson. Clarkson. Clarkson," they kept repeating over and over.

"Clarkson," they said louder, with authority, yanking my arm.

"Gah!" I screamed, snapping awake, and nearly falling out of my chair.

"*Shh!*" snapped a librarian from the opposite end of the room.

"Clarkson, you okay?" someone said, softly shaking my shoulder.

I looked to them; my vision was blinded by the sudden burst of light that went into them. I squinted my eyes to make out who it was. It was Mr. Martin.

He was sitting next to me in the same garb he wore when I first met him. He was leaning on the table, looking dry, but had tracked wet footprints in.

"Didn't mean to startle you so much," he whispered.

"I—" I started, but yawned, covering my mouth with my hand. "Sorry. It's okay. Had a weird dream."

"I bet, looking at what you're reading here," he said softly, pointing at the microform film's case.

Colonial Urban Legends was written on a piece of scotch tape that was pasted over a blank, square cardboard box. I chortled softly at myself. I was about to say something when a short woman with glasses came over to us.

"Sorry to interrupt you two, but it is currently eight fifty-five. We'll be closing in five minutes," she said in a soft, beautiful voice.

"Okay, thank you, ma'am," Mr. Martin said.

She walked away. I hoped my drowsiness could explain my staring. I felt embarrassed when Mr. Martin snapped his fingers in front of my eyes. He huffed out a laugh when I turned back to him, cheeks red.

"Anyways," I started, "what are you doing here?"

"Theresa said this is where I could find you. Hope she gets over her headache," he said, readjusting himself.

I nodded at his remark, smiling uncomfortably.

"I came to apologize about what I said the other day. I don't expect you to forgive me," he said.

"It's all good, Mr. Martin. I was more mad at myself than anything else. Ended up letting it all out when I shouldn't have."

"Well, don't let your anger swallow you. Stop by Smitt's office tomorrow. I need to talk to all three of you. Theresa and Ms. Smitt already know," he said, patting my shoulder as he stood up.

I watched him with suspicion as he walked out, taking his umbrella from a bucket at the door. I fluttered my eyes and turned back to the microform area. The microfilm was stopped about halfway through its roll, on a painting titled "The Foreigners Casket." There was a brief synopsis to the right of it.

"This tale comes from the ancient Lenape, Delaware, Susquehannock, and Iroquois people, one a few examples of cross-cultural myths. Three foreigners washed ashore on the banks of the Susquehannock River with a casket, and the Native peoples guided them into the Appalachian Mountains to seal the casket away."

I don't remember much—really anything—that happened since I got to the library. Hell, I didn't even remember going there. On the desk in front of me was my small note pad and written on it was a list of three people deceased, and next to them was three people born. Mostly men. Flipping through the notes, this stretched back to 1681. Further back than what this library would have records for. I snapped my head back to the door, looking for Mr. Martin, and then back to my pad. The latest entry on the pad was my father.

A rage rushed over me. I snapped back to the door to see my oldest sister standing outside of the glass. I blacked out.

When I awoke this time, I was in my bed. I shot up and flicked on the light on my nightstand behind my head. Something grabbed by wrist, a small claw digging into it. I breathed a deep sigh as my cat was lying on the pillow next to where my head was. He looked at me, smiling, purring. I laid back down, keeping the light on, waiting until exhaustion forced me to sleep.

CHAPTER 18

RADON

KORD

"It has an atomic mas of two hundred twenty-two and is the eighty-sixth element on the periodic table," I said, holding in the button on the walkie, knowing I was speaking into static. "It is a colorless, odorless, and tasteless noble gas. Don't let the name fool you either—there is nothing noble about this radioactive gas. Radon is the second leading cause of lung cancer in the United States, and roughly forty percent of homes in Pennsylvania possess dangerous levels of the element." I drug a rock through the dirt, drawing a big Rn inside a square.

"Radon itself cannot cause hallucinations, but it can worsen mental illnesses. For no particular reason, let's assume the illness of anxiety. Let's also assume that this anxiety started to affect this individual when they were no more than a child. Assume, as well, that this anxiety was as severe as you might imagine. Now assume that you take everything you're imagining and project it in front of you.

"Imagine a scenario or scene that can happen from a simple action. Think of the worst and most grotesque happening.

Have that image? Walk in a child's shoes. A child who is unaware that their subconscious is knowledgeable of the worst things that can happen to it, though the child has not witnessed it.

"That child now sits in the corner of the classroom, crying," I said and drew a long breath. "His classmates sit motionless in their hard rubber seats with bolted aluminum legs. They stare at the child screeching in his confined space—that child not seeing what they see. No. For him, there is no classroom. The room is filled with darkness, tunneling his vision into two pinpoint irises, choking him, and the only light comes from the glow of that behind the thick smoke. The backdraft covers him, and he believes he's burned, feeling the heat, but in reality, he's fine."

I rolled my neck from my left shoulder to my right, keeping my eyes closed. A shiver shook my spine, and I dropped my rock next to my flashlight. I was unsure where Raef went, but I knew he was listening somewhere.

"At home, it's even worse. He sits in his room, staring at the man in the corner. He knows not if the man is real or fake; he knows only that he's scared. The doctor says it's an imaginary friend. The father came for a look, but he didn't stay long. The man's stare looks real. The sound sounds real. The touch: real. The smell of the man: real. The child closes his eyes and counts to ten. The man doesn't leave. The fear in this child rises till he blacks out and dreams.

"It would not be till this child's preteen years that the house had its second ever radon test, and the results came in at three thousand six hundred forty-nine picocuries per liter. The highest ever recorded reading was in Lehigh County, Pennsylvania at three thousand seven hundred fifteen picocuries per liter. The US Environmental Protection Agency requires action at four picocuries per liter. After the house was purified, the man went away.

"I think I have discovered why this cave was closed up to start with. There is radon in here. I cannot taste it. I cannot see it. I cannot smell it. But I can feel it. The instability of my mind increasing without a reason I can fathom. The lightheaded feeling I'd get sitting in my bed, right before I saw him. And guess what. I am staring now at that man I saw in my room all those years ago. His shoulders are still as square as I remember."

I leaned back against the wall of the cave. Water dripped from the stalactites above me onto my head. I kept my eyes on the figure in front of me. I had always referred to this shadow as a male, but I guess it's more accurate to call it a thing.

"When I was little," I continued, "I let fear dictate my actions and my speech. Fear controlled my anxiety. I had no control of myself, no control of surroundings, no control of anything, and I could never think straight. I felt guided to a destination. It was so dark then, and a toxic lie, a smoke, filled my lungs. It wasn't our state's precious coal, it was almost sulfur but not quite it. I was always choking on it as it bellowed around me and got sucked through my lungs. It hurt then, and it hurts now as that horned beast turns its ugly head to me. But I cannot die. I will not let *you* take me. Not again."

I gave a smug grin and huffed at the figure, scratching the bottom of my chin.

"Huh, yeah…but maybe…I am already dead. I do not necessarily remember entering deeply into the cave. Raef was leading me through here, rarely speaking. Even then, I do not recall what it is he told me. There was some sort of humming. Something reached out for me, but it didn't speak. But it told me something, like it was already in my mind. Did

I die when the rocks fell? Is that why Clarkson and Theresa left? Did I actually ever talk to them? You know, don't you?"

The edges of the figure blurred and fidgeted like waves of water as it tilted its head at me. A crinkling, crunching sound accompanied its spastic movements. It stood straight up and down like a cardboard cutout. I'll admit I was scared. This thing knew I was, but I wouldn't give it the satisfaction of showing it.

"Naw. That couldn't be. Clarkson has been my friend for far too long to do that. Leave with no tears, that is. And Theresa, his sister? She likes me too much to do that either. Not in a romantic or sexual way, mind you, but in a friendly manner…I think. I see her as a friend, and I believe it's a mutual feeling but I dunno. Either way, she's like my sister and I ain't from West Virginia," I said and shrugged.

I picked at my nails, looking away from the encroaching shadows.

"It would also be nice if my grandmother didn't constantly ask me about her with that wink in her eye. Like, come on. She is my best friend's sister. It would be too weird. At least, for me. It's fine for others it seems, but I guess it depends on… Nev'mind. "

I quit picking at my nails.

"Alrighty, seriously, I don't know where I am. Do *you*? *You* don't, do *ya*? This isn't a new development; I know, but I feel lost more than usual. There is a massive weight on my feet, but I feel no weight anywhere else. I can feel stuff like my pack, my shirt, my arms, and my ugly mug. What do I do now, then? Where am I going?"

I fought as hard as I could, but something compelled me to say it. I tried so hard. My face folded and scrunched in on itself. My nose began to run, and there was pressure behind my eyes I last felt as a child. Something else. Something else had to be said. I didn't want to hear anything this thing might say after years of silence, and worse, I didn't want to face silence with it.

"Okay!"

I clapped and rubbed my hands together, then vigorously rubbed my face.

"Let's make sense of this situation. I have to still be in the cave, and…and I can't be dead. 'Cause I just touched my nose. I feel numb in my face, but that's good, I hope, because at least I have some feeling back. My dude, this is weird. My legs, they're asleep. *You* did this. I know it. I have to try and move them. If I concentrate, maybe I could…

"And lift…

"And lift…

"Alrighty, maybe swing…

"Swing…

"Goddammit.

"Oh, don't use the Lord's name in vain they say. Well, I'm not using it to decree my actions are justified by him when he denounces them."

My chest felt heavy, my lungs shallow, and the air thin. I felt like I was falling, actually falling. Not when you go to sleep, but if I jumped out of a plane. It was a long, long fall.

I looked away from the figure, and a wave of emotion came over me. There was a hard push against my chest, and a screaming in my ear. Whatever it was, was now on top of me. I clenched my fists and my eyes. The depression that had attacked me turned to anger, to fear. I started swinging.

I jumped to my feet, ignoring the pain of them being asleep. I kept my eyes closed as I stumbled about, hitting the air, the dripping water, the walls, myself. Hands scuffed and scratched. The blood flung from hand to hand. I then hit skin, and a cracking jaw yelled out in a loud snick on impact.

"Ow!" Raef said.

I opened my eyes and stared at him. I froze, speechless, my brows twitching.

"The hell is wrong with you?"

Fear. Fear was all I still felt. He backed up into the same spot where I saw that figure from my childhood. All those years ago. He grinned, the curling tips of his grin touching on the center of his forehead. Raef spoke that first word he said all those years ago.

"Hello?"

For a moment, my fear heightened. Then that fear turned to anger, hatred. I slipped my hand to a pocket, unbuttoned it, and out glided the flare gun.

"What are you doing?" Raef's grin stayed on his face.

I aimed it at him. Trying to control my breath.

"Kord, you're starting to worry me. Just put it away, okay?"

I did not budge.

"Kord, will you listen—"

I squeezed the trigger, and the flare shimmered a brilliant red. It flew toward him, and then through him. The flare hit the wall, then bounced once on the ground. Raef grunted. I opened the breech lock housing, and the cartridge was still inside like it didn't fire.

For a moment, there was nothing. Silence.

"Kord."

"Stay the fuck back."

"It would've been easier if you—"

I stomped my foot at him. I put away the flare gun and reached into my pocket, producing my pocketknife in my right hand, flicking out the blade. My pulse thudded against my ears.

"Pain is not fun, Kord. You should've listened."

"You are nothing to me, nothing."

"Nothing huh?" he said, standing in front of me.

I held the knife with both hands up to his jugular. Staring into his eyes, I saw someone who wasn't me staring back. The person I saw look just like Raef, but something was different. I didn't know what, and still don't know what, but this other person was pounding against their head with their own fists, occasionally opening their mouth to shout with nothing coming out.

"I am the force of all of the pain, the blunders, and the terror of man," Raef said, pressing against the knife.

"I'm not scared of you. I—"

He forced the knife through him, the blood flowing down the handle, down my hands, down my arms. My legs shook and buckled.

"I am not scared."

"Oh, dearest Kord," Raef said, grabbing my cheeks and holding my forehead to his. "I. Am. Fear."

I blacked out.

I woke up cold. It wasn't ice cold, nor was it the type of cold that you get when you ask someone out on a date, and they laugh while walking away with no answer. But the type of cold where you could wear a jacket over a lined flannel shirt. I had nothing. Not even my pack. But why was it cold? Have I traveled far enough to come across ice in this hellish darkness? Oh, well, maybe I am in hell, but if that's the case then I didn't think I'd be in the lowest circle.

There was nothing around me but a dark grayish-blue fog. I stood on top of ice. Though it was slick, I was still able to have a grip on the ice. Scared. Lost. In a literal fog. What else could I do? I chose what I usually did to keep my calm. I cleared my throat, took in a deep breath, and sighed. Then, I whistled. My lips dried almost every other note, and yet I kept whistling.

There was a deafening thud on the ice. I covered my ears and looked around in the fog. The thud happened again, and I fell to my knees. Again, the thud. My eyes became wet, and something came out of my ears.

Blood dripped onto the ice.

My reflection smiled up at me, laughing. To say I was disturbed is an understatement, I think. I didn't dare move, and my mouth went dry. Again, the ice started thudding. Right underneath me, it thudded.

It was not voluntary, and I didn't even realize it was me at first, but I screamed. Never before had I felt it this bad. I stammered back on my butt, and the ice started to crack.

A gray, seven-fingered hand emerged from the crack. It had a thumb on each side of the swirl-creased palm. It grabbed at me, but it couldn't reach. The fingers would slip and slide across the ice as the two thumbs would close in on each other and the other five fingers closed over top of them like a cage.

I tried to get up, but my hands kept slipping on the ice. The hand resubmerged and banged the ice more. The cracks grew and grew, little bits of ice launching into the air like dust. The hand burst through the ice, sending chunks flying. It stretched up into the sky like a skyscraper, and thundered back down on me, breaking the ice, dragging me under by my leg.

I kicked and slashed in the frigid water. I had never been able to open my eyes under water, and even now I struggled, but I opened them. Forced further into the open blue. I looked down, and a doppelgänger floated back up, dead as can be, to the ice.

I panicked, pushing my muscles to their limits to swim, but every stroke upwards only pushed me further down.

There was an all too familiar hiss. I jolted around, the quick bursts taking all my energy away with it. In the distance, it hissed again and reared its fangs. I had seen big cottonmouths before, but not one bigger than myself. The cottonmouth lunged at me, and my whole body was sucked into the beastly serpent. It was muddy inside.

Something stabbed into my back, and I braced for the worst. But my shirt stretched out, becoming taut, and I was thrown up to my feet. But every step I took to balance myself only made me slip around in the mud, flinging it everywhere. I could breathe, but my lungs burned like I swallowed bullets.

Some man with a bushy aristocratic mustache was yelling at me. He stood up straight, like some sort of general. I couldn't hear what he was saying—my ears ringing as I still caught my breath—but he mouthed my name over and over and over.

The ringing stopped; all sound stopped. The man blew a whistle, pointing to somewhere into the pea soup fog. His eyes pierced through me. Again, came the thudding, then came something hitting me like little stinging whips, tearing through me.

I tried to walk around, and each step felt like the finest of sewing needles pushed through me. Cold again, I felt my chest. My shirt gone and blood coating my skin. I fell to my knees, a ticking clock roared from somewhere.

Above me, on top of a breathtakingly beautiful white cliffside, stood Raef. He had a stick wedged underneath a boulder and was looking me dead in the eyes.

"Bye, piggy," he yelled down to me.

"Bye, Roger," I mumbled to myself.

The boulder took up more of my vision, so I closed my eyes and braced for it.

When I opened them, there was a small, dim light. And so, I felt dead, but I wasn't. I was moving, but not through my own fruition. Something pushed me, holding my shoulders. The light grew larger and larger as my feet forced me forward. Though still dim, I could see I wasn't alone. There were people shuffling in a line to a set of monstrous gates.

Hot, so hot.

A tall, bearded man drug around a large gold bell and a hammer with him. He had no shirt on, but he wore torn pants. He tried grabbing people's attention, but none of them even seemed to know he was there. Then he made eye contact with me, then to Raef. Raef's grasp on my shoulder loosened. Then the man spoke. Was he saying something to me? It sounded like Spanish. No, French. No…Basque? I'm still not quite sure. The only thing I was sure of was that it was hot.

Very hot.

It felt like hell.

CHAPTER 19

A PARADE OF DAMNED SOULS

KORD

A parade of damned souls marches forward. Each know what they have done, and each is begging for their appropriate punishment. All are screaming. All are weeping.

Except for me. For as I trudge forward, I do not weep. For as I trudge forward, there is no begging that escapes my lips. For as I trudge forward, I am at a slower pace. For as I trudge forward, the gates of hell stand wide and its torches' flames lick toward us and directly at me. Upon rocks, the princes watch; on a throne of smoke and ice, the Lord of Hell watches. Their eyes pierce us all and make the judgement for our damnation. Then those around me, all naked and bare, vanish without my care. Then, I am alone. Still, I trudge forward. I feel like I have been here forever, but I know I haven't, and someday I will probably return.

* * *

The gates ahead of me closed. A hand slowly dropped onto my shoulder with wind beneath it blowing against my neck and my face like an icy winter. But the placement was gentle, and the hand boney. I had no control of my physical actions, for I turned without care. I did not fear.

It kept telling me not to fear. Behind where I stood was the same Thing that I had been running from throughout the cave, and what Raef made me fear even more. Though the pale white face had blank eyes, it looked at me. Though it had no physical body, I felt its weight. Though it had wings to fly, it never did in my presence. And though it had no feet nor legs nor the body I mentioned, something told me it preferred to walk.

And that is what we did. We walked. It made no footsteps in the dirt, but there were two tracks. I call it dirt, but through my boots I could know just how soft it was. How plush, how warm, how odd it was. The dirt filled me with sorrow for people I didn't even know, and yet I felt their pain like it was my own.

And behind me, the princes and their lord stared. The yellow eyes they all possessed punctured and stabbed me, my heart and mind ached, but I was pulled forward.

I focused on the gate once more, and my heart sank. The last to enter was an older man I knew, a father of a friend, who looked into my eyes and his weeping stopped. A drop of cider dripped from his lips. The ground became a solid rock.

This figure guiding me entered into a familiar buff-colored boat and beckoned me in. For why it did not speak, I do not know. I entered. I sat. This Thing and I studied each other. And the shores were no more.

Kord, it spoke without speaking.

"Yes?"

Are you hungry?

"I...I don't know. I do not think I am," I said, putting my hands in my lap.

It cocked its head, and it smiled. Reaching its hand over the right side, into what looked like water beneath us, it waited, staring down. Whatever this liquid was parted like a fluid gel around its arm. It reminded me of half-melted ice cream because it was...well, it just did. It pulled its hand out, holding a fish by the rear fin, after many others had gone by.

I do believe you have a plate.

My hands were already reaching without thinking and pulling out my mess kit. I disassembled it and reached out with the plate and the fish was laid upon it. Still holding the fish by the fin, the Thing, this Being, pulled the fin across the fish, making a new fish. This new fish was placed back into the ice-cream water and shook before swimming off again. I became hungry and ate.

I would cut a slice of the fish, eat it, and go to slice off another. All the while, it watched me. I finished half of the fish before I had realized.

"Who are you?" I asked after finishing a bite.

It did not answer.

"Are. Are you God?" I asked before taking another bite.

No, it answered very quickly, almost before I had even finished the question.

A long pause was filled only by the sound of calmly flowing water from the ice-creamesque river. I cut another piece of fish.

Nor am I the Son, it said as I finished the fish.

"I take it that your name or who you are does not matter then, just what you are?"

It nodded and took my entire mess kit, dipping it in the water. It came out clean and dry.

"And I take it that it is for my own responsibility to know or discover who you are?" I asked, taking the mess kit back and putting it away.

Again, it nodded. And again, we sat in a long, comfortable silence. It pointed at my sack, and the boney hand was replaced with a small, soft, feminine one for this brief moment. I took it off, placing it in my lap, still focusing on the hand. It turned up its palm and uncurled the soft-looking fingers. I hung the bag by the strap in its hand. Its grasp around it was slow, but it was unshaking, firm, and stable. It pulled the bag close, holding it tightly in a hug.

It unzipped the smallest full pocket, pulled out my Walkman and cassette. It was Simon and Garfunkel's *Bridge over Troubled Water*. Inserting the cassette, pressing the play button, it started up right on the song baring the same title. The Being didn't plug in the headphones for the device, but just held it in its hands, and I could hear it.

We floated further down this river, just listening to the music. It was peaceful, and I felt happy for the first time in this whole debacle.

A shore emerged on both sides of us. Fog rolled over the shores on both sides of the boat. On our right was a forest. Pines and maples stood tall as mighty oaks and regal birches watched with sorrow over their sister aspens. Bushes dotted this forest along with vines and grasses sprinkling and dancing over the floor. To our left was a barren landscape of clean, smooth, flat shale. A figure walked, at the speed of our boat, on the shore. This figure had its hands behind its back, and it held its head high. It was Raef. He looked to us, and the Being put its reskeletonized hand on my shoulder.

I wanted to run after him. I wanted to kill him. But the Being did not let me leave.

Calm, Kord.

"Why should I cal—"

Because I am telling you it is okay.

I looked to the Being and tried to calm down.

Do not feed into the anger, hate, or fear. They all end up being the same thing: death.

"What is Raef?"

Fear can be one of the biggest liars there is if you let it. You can trust fear to tell you what it is. Fear is fear itself. It is not wholly good nor wholly evil. Fear is fear itself. Fear can be a tool to help you and a tool to tear you down. Fear is fear itself.

"I don't understand what you mean," I said, changing my glance to the muddying water around us. "Why do you keep saying 'fear is fear itself'?"

Your instinctive fear is a good fear, giving you caution when something is not right. But if you do not think or ponder on as to why fear has stopped you, then you let it guide you into darkness. Do not let fear keep you from learning, from growing, from loving. Using fear as a special tool to think wisely is living above fear. Those around you will let fear guide them at times they shouldn't. Those that let fear take over their lives will stop at nothing to make others fear with them. It is easier to live in fear than it is to live above fear. Fear is fear itself.

"How do I stop fear then?"

You don't. You use it as a tool to learn. But do not use it as a tool to control.

"Is it possible to come out of living in fear?"

Quite. It is not easy. It will be hard. It will be painful. It will make you bleed. But you will bleed away bad blood. It takes love, knowledge, and common sense to leave that life. You cannot use hate; that is fear's own game.

"Am I living in fear?"

Ask and test for yourself. You must be the one willing, the one wanting, and the one working to leave a life of fear. You must realize and recognize it first. Notice when you noticed him.

The boat came to a halt. There was a clear passageway through the forest, an opening clear to a cave entrance. I knew what had to be done. I had to enter. I stood slowly in the boat and kept my eyes on the entrance. Slowly, I grabbed my bag from the boat, keeping my eyes off of Raef, who was still looking at me.

I shook him from my mind and stepped onto the shore, the soil firm and damp. I breathed in deeply, held it, and let it out slowly form my nose. I put my bag over one shoulder, then the next, then took my Walkman and plugged in the headphones. By this point, Simon and Garfunkel had finished their song, and Vera Lynn was singing "We'll Meet Again."

I walked into the forest, through the clearing. The soil crunched beneath my feet as the canopy above me grew thicker. I turned, and the Being was gone, and Raef was still on the shale. I gave him no thought and kept walking. As the song played, a pep in my step started to emerge. I was free; for once during this whole episode, I wasn't weighed down at that moment. In fact, I was quite joyful.

Until something moved across my foot. The face of a cottonmouth stared right into my eyes. It flew off with a kick as I breathed heavily and caught my breath from the shock. The music stopped.

"Oh, Kord," the voice came through my headphones.

"No."

"We're not done yet, Kord. Not until you leave my domain."

"Then I will find the exit, Raef," I said, turning back around to him.

"Is that so? Perhaps, some "Summer Wine" before you go?"

He took a step upon the water, and he walked across it. I took one step backward. Then another. And Raef took them in sync with longer strides. Yet still, I backed up more and more, and he got closer and closer. Fear, the unwanted and successful seducer, had me in his own game. An intolerable game. I clenched my eyes shut, shaking my head, and stopped moving. Raef did not.

"Don't be afraid, Kord," he said then bellowed as he got closer and closer.

"Piss off!" I shouted, running for the cave.

His steps echoed behind me, but I ran faster. I dove into the cave, and its entrance shrank. Raef picked his pace up more and more. Huffing to get in before it shut. Above the entrance was a large letter *D* and "twenty-nine." The cave shut, and I was alone. I closed my eyes, and heaved, catching my breath.

I awoke on my back where I'd confronted Raef originally, coal dust coating me and my clothes. No Walkman. Raef standing above me.

"You are going to remember something for me, Kord. You will not like it."

CHAPTER 20

MEYER THE PLANNER

?

I had followed Kord for most of my time now, and to take a break and witness what will happen to my dear sweet friend, Chinkwe Meyer would be the best possible treat. Pulling some strings behind the scenes, it was finally time that I might be able to escape my quagmire, to get the justice that I deserve. Two of the three that put me in here would finally fight each other till I was out. What better way to rid myself of them than to have them turn on each other?

Meyer sat in his study, sealing himself away, on a large comfy velvet chair, he was leaning over his knees, his chin resting on his fists. He wore light brown khakis, a blue, almost denim, shirt with a black undershirt. His hair was slicked back. It was unlike him to grow it out. Must have been just for me. He had hot tea on the chair next to him. The light of the room was a silent, somber candle. It was safe to assume he knew I was with him in there. He bounced his leg.

"Raef! Take a seat across from me," he said, sitting back up in his chair.

"That would spoil the fun, Meyer."

"You have a flaw in your deal, one easily exploited."

His eyes were closed, clenched tightly together. I was intrigued now. Meyer pinched the flame on the candle, silencing it. I walked from the dark corner and took a seat across from him. Meyer snapped his fingers and it lit again, but it was much dimmer. His gaze was intense. Hands fisted on his lips. I gave him a cocky grin. I knew I was, but I had earned the right to be, or at least I thought so. Even the rooms around him he had let grow dim to let me in.

"Raef."

"Meyer."

"It has been a while since I've seen you in person."

"Hehe, likewise, sir."

He sipped his tea and rested his arm.

"Meyer, you said something about my deal being faulty, I do believe."

"Yes, Raef. You see, the agreement was that I could get into the position I am in now, and in return I would help you get out and be free."

"That is indeed part of it."

"Yes, and I have been able to do great things for this land. Hell, Philly is safe to walk in at night now, and the city is no longer being burned down when the football team wins or loses a game. You have helped, that is true. And the spot is secure for reelection this fall."

"Quite, quite. Um, Meyer, the error of the deal?"

He smiled and grabbed his round glasses from his shirt pocket and put them on. He looked at me and took another sip of tea before looking back into the darkness.

"You see, Raef. I could not interfere with you getting out. I would play my magic and you would have someone to latch onto to escape."

"Correct," I said, looking at him, still intrigued but now increasingly annoyed that he would not get to the point.

"If I were to order all officers away from the caves, it would hurt my image, but I would recover with a very easy spiel about safety for all the officers over one person and it was a great loss, yadda yadda yadda. I have to keep up the image that something is happening, so, if I were to give that order, then that would also break the deal. And I would no doubt be killed, correct?"

"Indeed."

"But what would happen, pray tell, if I passed clues off to another? And do pray tell if I just had people search the waters? You've helped in keeping information hush-hush for the most part."

"Doesn't break the deal. You told Smitt, I know. And you wanted me to know because you knew she would."

"If I were to simply let them go in, then they would get lost, and that would help no one. If I were to do anything else along the lines of preventing Kord from getting out, then that would not help. You have to lead him out through your own means; thus, you can attach to him."

I nodded.

"Raef, I am about to break our deal in a way that doesn't break it," he said, smiling. "I will surely die, I know, but our secrets in the Appalachians have been kept secret since the days of the Lenape Delaware. Subsequently when I had shed my old self and started looking like this."

I stiffened in the chair. Staring him down.

"Meyer, I do not believe that there is any way to break it. The only way for something to happen is if Martin got involved and did it himself by going in. You two have not been in contact nor enjoyed each other's company for some time," I said this and relaxed myself.

"True, which is why I used Kord's friends." He paused for another sip of tea and looked at me.

"How does using his friends lure in Martin?"

"Any time the mountains have been involved in anything, he's gotten involved, especially with the caves. This time would be no different. I knew Kord had close friends from the start. His friends would stop at nothing to get him back. He is family to them, as many friends can become.

"And there's Clarkson, the hot-tempered short one. We both know that when someone fights Martin, Martin will fight back harder, no? So, what better way than to have the two fight?

"Have Clarkson push Martin's buttons. Martin will push back at buttons Clarkson didn't even know he had. Martin has been touchy these past twenty-two years; especially since our third had broken our vows, settled down and had a family. Martin drove that man to drink, I swear."

"You think I didn't plan for something like that, Meyer? Remember the other day? When you let yourself get carried away?"

"Oh, save me from your tales, Raef. How does what I did have any relevance to this?"

"They're going to get you, but I can stop them. It will be a very painful experience, Meyer. Not just physically."

"Blah, blah, blah, Raef. I die, so what? Just like Martin, I'll come back."

"Everything that you have built up, will be torn down. They will find that phone and go after the siblings, too. The blood of all of you would be on your hands."

"Martin was the strongest of the three of us. I was easily swayed, but I was the most clever in planning, negotiating, and you knew that, Raef. Really, I guess I have the silver tongue. If you kill me, the world will know what is in the caves. I will tell them."

"How will Martin be able to save all three?"

The candle's flickering light now threatened to burn the room. It licked against Meyer's face.

"Martin is stronger in spirit than body, literally. All he has to do is kill himself. He will guide Kord out of the caves and be able to turn around in time to save Theresa and Clarkson. Or," he raised a finger after finishing his tea, "you kill me, Kord gets out, and you fight Martin. If those three friends unite, I predict that means you would have gotten out anyways and will be forced to keep your word on that."

Once he finished speaking, there was pounding on the door. The sound coming through the vents. I hushed the candle.

"Raef, that of course will be if we—Martin, the siblings, Kord, and I—succeed. But remember, if you break your deal, and Kord does get out, then well… Oh, why am I telling you? You already know."

His smug grin grew across his face. He tapped his fingers together, staring me down. The pounding on the door happened again.

"You already broke the deal, Meyer."

"But have I? If I recollect, I haven't done anything yet."

My brows slopped inwards like a cliff above my wide eyes. He had to have done something, otherwise—

"Raef, what does the wall of the cave, with the fog light and your puppet, say?"

I didn't answer him. I wouldn't play his game while he played mine.

"Hello, Raef?"

"Go to hell, Meyer. Go to hell and burn with Sherman!"

"Oh, Raef, I love you too."

The door to the home was broken down. He stuck out his tongue at me. It slithered out between his teeth like a moccasin moves through the water. I made a quick realization, one that I should've made many years ago. His tongue was silver.

CHAPTER 21

SAFETY FOR SPEED

KORD

"Buckled?" my mom asked me.

"'Yep!' I told her so enthusiastically.

"The oh so familiar Ford Bronco I-I. The seats were beige, beat up, worn and torn. Mom had a solution that involved just putting seat covers over them. The floor was brown, dirty and stained. Removable floor mats were the solution to that. Mom liked to keep the inside as clean as possible. The passenger side door had some troubles latching from time to time, but a good slam usually would do it.

"I don't remember how old I was, but I was young. Didn't need a booster seat. The pleasant aroma of the Eat 'n Park's bakery treats was still present on her clothes. Where was I when she picked me up?

"Let's see. Oh yeah, I was at my friend's house in Country Meadows. That's a trailer park over on the other side of Middlesex Township. I had a handful of friends from there then. I had just told them bye through the car's window. To get home, we'd take Bernheisel to Sherwood to Hollowbrook, cross North Middlesex onto Beagle Club. Then onto West Middlesex Drive. And the corn or wheat, whatever it was, it was tall. It was fall. Almost time for harvest

"It was cold that night. Very cold. The sun had fallen, and the moon had risen. At least, what we could see through the clouds and fog. There was rain. Good bit of it. We had our lights on. We were stopped at what was, and still is, a three-way intersection with Wolf's Bridge Road. Back then, the bridge was still in use.

"I was so happy to tell Mom of what we had done that day at school—the test I passed, and what I had learned. We were learning about physics—how a bigger object can move a smaller object—and the teacher demonstrated it using little diecast cars and some track. Ironic, I guess."

I shook my head and looked at Raef. The corners of his mouths did not curl. He did not change his breathing. His ears did not twitch. His eyes though, I could read those eyes. He was enjoying every bit of it.

"Why am I remembering this all of a sudden?" I asked him.

"Why are you asking me, Kord?"

"'Cause, I haven't thought of that night for a long time. Would've enjoyed it if I didn't have to."

"Doesn't the human mind just not have an interesting way of remembering things?"

"Don't give me that bullshit, Raef. What are you doing?"

"Finish the story, Kord."

I wanted to chuck a rock at him. I couldn't feel my right arm, but something was telling me not to move it anyways. And I didn't dare take my sight from that bastard. So, I used my left arm, and threw something at him, something jagged, sharp. Sharp...

"Sharp. A sharp is a musical term for going up a half step on a note. It is possible to have a double sharp, even triple sharps. I think they're stupid though. Just as stupid as not driving with your lights on in the fog, early morning, the rain, at night."

Raef cocked his head at me unamused.

"The pain was sharp. One moment I was cheery, the car filled with my ecstatic voice and the static-filled music from the radio. The next? Crunching. Cracking. Metal screaming at me. Another car had been coming up the hill, and Mom couldn't see 'em. Other than seeing him last second, I don't remember much of the initial collision.

"I looked up when the spinning stopped. Something was dripping on me. I was soaked. I wasn't even on the side that was hit, but I was thrown from the car. The passenger door went—" I made a whistling sound followed by popping my lips, dragging my finger in an arc through the air. I checked to see if Raef got the gist. He rolled his head to the other side.

"Clear from the car. I don't even know where it went. Somewhere into the fields of tall stalks, I assume. The Bronco wrapped around a stop sign. The car that hit us left a near-perfect imprint on the Bronco like it was silly putty. Bits of the front were here and there; a headlight laid next to me. The lights from the car were still on.

"It was a while till I noticed the blaring of another distinct car horn. A much higher pitch. The pattering of the rain in the muddy field was the only thing that was talking to me."

"And what did it say to you, Kord?" Raef asked. He was now probably no more than a foot from my face, perfect distance for my fist.

I waited, contemplating my next action, and continued the story, "A voice. It said—"

"Get up, Kord," Raef finished with a whisper.

"So, I did…as you said. I got up. My legs were sore, and my wrist, my right wrist, it was the sharp pain. I went back to the car, oil pooling and running off of the road. And then an even sharper pain hit. My mom. Mom…"

Raef was even closer, putting a hand on my head.

My vision darkened. I tried to push him off, but something in my hand was heavy, weighing it down, and I couldn't do a thing about it.

"Finish the story. Remember what happened."

"I got to the car. The steering column had been shot up through her. Shards of glass dug into her face. One piece had logged itself into her chin. It kept fogging up.

"The higher pitched honking stopped. I waved to the other car, but they drove off in a panic. Under the passenger seat was an old CB radio meant for emergencies. And well, it was an emergency. I thought so at least. What do you think, Raef?"

He didn't respond, but he had closed his eyes. The world around me was darker.

"I plugged the radio in the cigarette lighter port, and the thing had a weak signal. I had no idea how to use, but I just squeezed the button and started squeaking into it like a mouse. I cried, and I cried, and if felt like there was a hand soft on my shoulder. I don't know whose, but I didn't care.

"I cried into the radio, it was still on, the button pressed, but no one responded to me. Nothing but static. My mom's cell phone buzzed in the cup holder. It had no notification, but it buzzed."

The weight in my hand became more and more apparent as I remembered the CB static from the car.

Raef moved a hand to my neck. "Part of the sweet, 'Summer Wine,' Kord. Just sweet 'Summer Wine,'" he mumbled in a guttural voice.

"Do you even know what that means?"

"Don't think about it too much, Kord."

I didn't have the strength nor the want to argue with him.

"The rain picked up, and it became a downpour. I called 911. I was still crying as the operator tried to calm me down. I gave her the information through spits, sniffles, and bursts of inaudible whimpering. I looked up to my mother, and the glass stopped fogging. Her eyes became that of glass.

"Surprisingly, the radio and cassette player still worked. 'We'll Meet Again' played. And I supposed we did. Ain't it ironic, Raef. For as much fear and sorrow as you tried to put into me?"

I started to laugh, and Raef stared directly into me with dark, black eyes. Something that would make Yevhen Hrebinka, a Russian-Ukrainian poet, write a demented sequel to "Dark Eyes."

"Perhaps it was that someone was listening over that CB though, but they just didn't respond. And maybe they were just in the area. For the first person to arrive to the scene wasn't an officer, EMT, or firefighter. It was Mr. Sherman."

Raef snickered at the mention of the name.

"And guess what he always had on him, being such an enthusiast?"

"What was that, Kord?" Raef asked, tightening his grip, a light in his eyes.

Now he was playing my game.

"A walkie-talkie."

I squeezed the walkie in my hand and swung hard and fast. The plastic cracked against his temple, chipping off a corner of the hard plastic.

"Gah!" Raef screamed.

He rolled right off of me, and I on top of him. Punching into him four more times. As strong as he seemed, he was actually quite weak.

Then the walkie had static come over it.

"Ksss, K-Kord. Kssssss, Kord!" Clarkson's squeaky voice came over in a whisper.

Raef laughed, his nose bleeding, and kneed me right in the stomach.

"Kagh!" I blurted out.

"Kord!" Clarkson squeaked again like a mouse.

Raef kicked me again, right in the nose.

"Kord, where are you at?" The mouse squeaked again.

Raef took a swing, but I ducked and gave him another blow right in the gut. In this world, it might be his domain, but it's not his realm. I grabbed his head, drove my knee into it twice, and threw his head down into the coal. I stomped it, his head flattening out, the brains flying, getting stuck on my boot. He was a bug under my shoe. I could still hear his yelps and his laughing.

An eye rolled from the socket and halted looking right at me. Many more, many, many more followed. And they were looking at me, blinking independently of each other. I started stomping and squishing them. The floor was covered. Still, one by one, then two by two, and three by three, I squished them. The floor turned from a solid rock to a mushy, foul-smelling sludge. Like…overly…moist…I threw up into it, stepping out from the floor.

"Kord! Are you there?" Clarkson's squeaking voice echoed from the walkie.

"Y-yeah," I finally responded, "some messed up shit is going on."

"It's about to get worse for y'all."

"How the hell could it?"

"Ha-hah-haaa," Raef growled through the walkie.

I spiked the walkie as if it were a football, and I had just made a game-winning Superbowl touchdown. It shattered and splintered, sparking, bits flying every which way. The hard plastic acted like it was some cheap, thin shell that was molded and produced from a low-budget factory. I grabbed my lantern as a low-bellowed rumble filled the cave like it was a stomach.

I stammered around, at first, but I began running. I jumped over the mac and cheese floor, ignoring what it actually was, and kept booking it. There was another deafening rumble, rocking the cave even more. Sounded almost like dynamite, and if it were, it would leave this cave burning for years. But as for the dust floating around me and throughout the corridor, it would go up in a near instant.

Forward, not looking back, I ran. My light bounced ahead of me, but it kept shining off the black coal. A blast went off, and it must have been close, because it made me tumble head over heels and roll onto my side. I coughed and spat up dust that got in my lungs. I crawled desperately to get out of the dust, even over something lumpy and wet on the ground. It smelled like death. A piece of the ceiling behind me crumbled into the cavern, kicking up even more dust.

Climbing my way back to my feet, I took a handful more steps, clearing the worst of the dust, and took a long drink from my canteen. I shined my light ahead of me and saw an open part of the cave that had some illumination. I had no other choice. The floor squished beneath me. The wall was on fire. And after inspecting the other tunnels, they all had spider webs. There was a thick drumming hum.

Welcome back, Kord.

"Indeed, Kord. Welcome back," his damn voice echoed in the open room.

CHAPTER 22

THE TOMB

KORD

The fire on the wall was still burning bright, and the star shined brilliantly over the chamber. Before Raef took me down the tunnels, going in a circle, I almost expected to hear "The only way up, is down"—*As Above So Below* is an underrated movie in my opinion.

Raef watched me from atop the ledge side, smiling, holding a marionette in his hands. He shook it around. It was blank, like an unmarked potato sack. I held my lantern in my left hand, walking over the mushy floor, to just below Raef. He seemed to be focused on something back in the tunnel. I turned back and saw nothing. I shrugged my shoulders and threw the battery powered lantern up on top of the ledge. I squatted and hopped up, grabbing the rock with both hands, and pulled myself up to sit on the edge.

I took off my backpack, setting it next to me, and took out a granola bar from a pouch. Raef stood, staying transfixed on the tunnel I had walked out of. I took a bite out of the bar, its loud crunch breaking the trance Raef was in. He was puzzled, his brows furled, eyes shooting between me and the tunnel.

"The hell ya lookin' at?" I asked him.

He didn't respond, and I didn't care enough to ask again. I sat there, collecting my breath while eating the granola. He played around with the marionette, noticeably upset that it was blank. I breathed in deeply and coughed up black coal-covered mucus. It looked like sludgy snow from the street. I cleared my throat and spat, breathing better after I had. I coughed and then finished the granola bar.

Raef still shot his head back and forth as if a security camera. It wasn't until I rezipped my pack and punctured a juice box did he look at me. For once, he was the one that looked scared, and that made me smile for some reason. I don't know why, but I smiled, sucking on the straw to the apple juice like my life depended on it, and then I began to laugh. I couldn't fathom why that would make him scared, little did I know, that it wasn't my obnoxious slurping.

"It happened," he finally stated.

"What's that?" I asked.

"Follow me."

"Raef. So far," I started, pointing at him on every syllable, "when I've followed you, I have been faced with my own personal hell. So, in recognition of this evidence, kindly piss off."

"Please, Kord, just trust me this once."

"Why?"

"Because *I* am scared."

MR. MARTIN

The muted morning light was just poking through the trees over the mountain. The mountain to which so much of my life I was forced to study. It was still raining, most roads having been shut down as Meyer and the governor issued a travel warning over flooding. Some chose to ignore that, but, for the most part, the streets were quiet. The wind was quiet even though I could feel it hitting my face, along with the sharp, piercing rain. There was almost no sound. The way I could tell if I was awake or asleep.

The rain dug into the ground like thousands of little picks at once making a railroad, slamming into the ground on their own beat. The dirt was a muddy mess, but it was still firm enough to walk on—like it always is when I need it to be. The same way that Clarkson could make it in his dreams, manipulate the world to be what he wants, what he needs.

The little Napoleonic rat stood next to me. I casually lit a cigarette, smoking it with the rain pouring over my face. Clarkson held a letter in his right hand. His left hand held on to a blank gravestone. I don't think he could see me. He wore a pair of light cargo shorts, sandals, and a long rain jacket with its hood up. Normally, people would be crying whenever looking over a loved one's grave, and maybe the rain masked it, but his face wasn't red, it wasn't tight, and his eyes weren't puffy.

Theresa sat in a still-running car, watching her brother with annoyance. I tried to listen to what he was saying, but something else was talking to me telling me that I wasn't seeing a "now" but instead something that happened before.

Clarkson, taking the letter, stuffed it into the mud at the base of the gravestone. The quiet then turned to static. A soft static at first, but it grew and grew until a painful headache grew. Clarkson drug his feet back to the car, sitting on a towel-covered seat. He fastened his seatbelt and looked back. Through me to something else. I turned around, seeing something in the far-off trees. It was the same figure that I saw in the corn fields with Ms. Smitt. It was more opaque, and it had short shoulder-length hair. Its eyes were dark with little white dots in the center of each.

They drove off, the sound of the gravel moving catching my attention for a second, losing my eye contact with the thing in the trees. They drove slowly, vanishing before even leaving my eyesight, the world around me closing dark. For once, I wasn't in control of my dreams. The only light left came from a spotlight above me. Looking back to the grave, there was a woman sitting on the muddy dirt of what would truly be a grave if there were a casket. They looked right up at me while pointing at their gravestone.

Her eyes were blank, but I could feel the confusion, pain, and anger that they had. The little white dots were like little pinpoint tacks made for you to stare at them, letting yourself get lost in their static filled face. It seemed to know who, or at least what, I was. I followed its outstretched arm, to its seven-fingered hand. The blank stone wasn't so blank now, from 1993–2021.

I mumbled to myself, "Dammit Sherman."

CLARKSON

Theresa and I sat in Smitt's office, in the usual executive chairs, waiting on both Smitt and Mr. Martin. The rain pattered against the window, and the spot on the ceiling had more little black friends around it—the building showing its age with a poorly thatched roof. The map was still on Smitt's desk, still held down by the same unmoved objects. Blue and red pins held pages, photos, and sticky notes to the small corkboard on the wall.

Theresa twiddled her thumbs and hummed something. A sense of déjà vu rushed over me as the clacking of Martin's and Smitt's shoes in the hallway caught my attention. I looked up to see their shadows quickly moving across the hallway window shades, Martin following Smitt, but now there was a third, not making any distinct footing sounds. I nudged Theresa, motioning with my head to the approaching shadows. Theresa didn't seem at all troubled, just nodding at me. Understandable, I guess, it wasn't like we were the only ones in the whole building—it was the administrative center of Carlisle, after all.

The door flung open, Smitt walking in first, not holding the door, which swung back and was caught by Mr. Martin's face. Theresa and I both held in laughter as he paid no attention as to what just happened. That was two shadows accounted for. The third stood in the hallway, positioned as if looking right into the room through the curtains.

"Who's that?" I asked.

"Who's who?" Ms. Smitt asked in an annoyed tone.

I pointed to the shadow. "That."

Mr. Martin looked at me, his cheeks becoming red. He looked away for a second to the shadow, then back to me, sighing.

"Who's *what*?" Ms. Smitt asked, again annoyed.

"Nothing," Mr. Martin said, "It'll all be explained soon."

"Cabrón. Save the bullshit for yourself, Martin," Ms. Smitt said.

Theresa and I gave each other a subtle surprised look, never having seen her this mad before. Martin took the silver case out from his jacket, going through the motions of lighting a cigarette. But, when the lighter ignited, the flame was larger than usual. He was transfixed by it, like watching a movie. The cigarette first drooped from his lips then fell to the ground. He turned to the shadow outside.

"Mr. Martin," Ms. Smitt said, waving her hand directly in front of him. "Martin!"

"No soy sato. Take a seat, niña," Martin replied in a cold, direct tone.

He pointed to the seat behind her which moved on its own and scooped her off of her feet. Ms. Smitt was surprised to say the least, probably from Martin's use of Puerto Rican slang more than the self-moving chair. Martin flicked the zippo closed and put it back in his pocket, bending over and picking up the unlit cigarette. He inspected it before putting it behind his ear. He snapped his fingers, and a cart with a TV strapped on top of it rolled over to us. Martin pressed the power button and handed the remote to Theresa.

"Put it on any local news channel, please," he said, taking a seat on the corner of the table.

MEYER

And so, with Raef "gone," I sat alone in my study, listening to the banging vibrating throughout the house. The thudding of officers' feet thundered from upstairs. I don't have a big house, but I do have a basement that has a fairly hidden door. And until they find it, or I step out, they'll scan the whole house confused. I studied the noise, and that got harder as it grew quieter and quieter, being replaced with static.

"That you, Sherman?" I asked into the empty room.

The flame snuffed itself out. The only light came from two small white dots in the corner.

"I see," I said. "I shouldn't leave them that full of suspense, should I?"

The dots didn't say anything. I just drummed my fingers together. I stood up from the chair, not needing any light to know where the door was. I grabbed the knob and looked back to the two white dots. It wasn't Raef. It didn't feel like Sherman. I didn't know what it was. For the first time in a long while, I felt an anger filled with fear.

I turned the knob and opened the door, closing it firmly behind me. I walked up the creaky wooden stairs that were no more than the door's length away. Between each step, in the dark gaps, those two white dots watched me. I closed my eyes and continued up the steps, slowly opening the door to the first floor. I was greeted by two officers with their pistols drawn on me.

"At ease, boys. I'm unarmed," I joked, raising my hands.

CLARKSON

We watched the TV in disbelief as Meyer stepped from his house in handcuffs, the news camera zooming in on him struggling to focus. The field anchor described the events as they unfolded. Meyer walked with his head held high and legs stepping in unison with the two officers that flanked him, each with a hand on his forearm. Watching the whole thing unfold felt unreal. They didn't say why he was being arrested, but I assumed it was for hitting the one senator.

When trying to get him into the back of the cop car, I found it increasingly harder not to laugh. Meyer was a tall man, and the car door was short. They had to practically lie him down then fold up his feet just to get him in. Still, why he was being arrested was never said.

Martin cleared his throat as he turned off the TV. He pushed the cart out of the way and looked each one of us in the eyes. He watched the hallway, and the shadow was no longer there.

He took in a deep breath and sighed. "Listen up, I don't have much time, and you all need to know this. You might believe or not, or you can be like Smitt here and blow me off when I start the story.

"In the ancient world, before Rome had conquered it, there was a Kingdom of Twelve Tribes, Israel. From this area, the first of the Abrahamic religions, Judaism, was able to flourish. The original words that helped breathe life into this and many other ancient religions no longer exists, but that's not important yet. Many years later, and I mean many, Christianity rolls around.

"Now this religion had all sorts of branches from the get-go. One of these sects retreated into the deserts of North Africa, and from there, merged with a Judaic sect, and formed a sort of mini-Abrahamic religion, akin to the sizes of Samaritanism, Mandaeans, and Babism. We were a mix of Levanters, mostly Hebrews, Egyptians, Berbers and others from the Maghreb. It was under an era of having to keep secret, that this group traversed the Northern Coasts of Africa to what is now Morocco.

"Part of their belief was that the Antichrist is in the form of consciousness and not in man or from conception. This beast, if you will, manifests in person to person and will lie to stay alive. Furthermore, the Antichrist does his worst when more and more people fall for him. The only way to conceal him is by trapping him behind what we referred to as a carpenter's compass. Really it was the Greek Cross, the Star of David, and a moon that bears a striking resemblance to the Islamic Moon. The moon coming from the original lost words, supposed to be the face of God watching over us at night. The Ottomans started using the crest, and history tells the rest as to why you'd recognize it.

"Anyways. One of the members fell to him, to the Antichrist. They did the most and best they could to fight him. Ultimately, God damned the entire group off the mainland to the Canaries, then the Azores, and then the sea. Many of the group died on the islands and many of them starved with the Antichrist on board that ship, kept in a coffin with the compass-looking symbol.

"Upon one morning, a seagull perched on the bow, and they gave thanks that they did not perish on the journey, for no ship was yet suited for the open waters. With the thanks that was given, a command was given for them to not disembark until they had traveled a river and the ship crashed on rocks. Those that did not listen, died by riptides or were drowned—even the strongest swimmers.

"The ship rounded today's Virginia Beach and continued up the Chesapeake Bay. Disobeying our understanding of physics, the Susquehannock River's currents reversed. The ship ran aground many times but was swept back out and still traveled the river. One stormy day, it scratched against a rock next to an island roughly two klicks long, and eventually capsized on the shore near what's now Goldsboro.

"They were met on the shore by the Natives. The Natives were a warrior people but did not attack those carrying the coffin off the boat. There were now only a handful of them, and one was the Antichrist in the coffin.

"They followed the tribesmen up the trails until they reached the mouth of a cave that had the star. The party, now only three strong—not including the one in the coffin—and refusing any drink and food from the Natives until they were done, entered the cave. After entering, one of them turned to face the Natives, and spoke in their tongue:

> *Do not enter these caves, marked by this symbol.*
> *And do not let out anyone unless they shall bear our duty or witness us in full accordance with His will.*

"And so, it was done. Us three marked three true entrances and exits of the caves with a carpenter's compass and false ones with a directional compass. Was the only thing at the time we could think of, and it made sense to us to do it.

"The one that had been possessed in his subconscious stayed trapped in the cave, his name backward to what he is. The other three were trapped to walk the earth until the time came for them to take themselves into the Kingdom. One of them was a very nice lad, very talented, very courageous, but would drown on dry land and their death would cast a curse on their family. One was to possess two names foreign upon each other and able to project himself as two people. And the last one would fight like hell, be a legitimate bastard, but ultimately be unheard until many had died. Cryptic I know."

Martin took the cigarette out from behind his ear and took his zippo back out, lighting the death stick. He took a long draw and then coughed it out with such pain that even I felt it. Smitt crossed her arms and rolled her eyes.

MEYER

I leaned back in the uncomfortable plastic seat, looking out the window. None of us spoke, and to be honest, I am surprised that I wasn't arrested sooner. Sure, I might not have been the one doing wrong, but I was the one to throw a punch. If I were found guilty, oh well.

Though none of us spoke, I was tempted to ask them to drive a bit slower over the potholes in the road—practically a staple of the roads in Pennsylvania. It was as if they purposefully drove over each one. Every time they did, the metal cuff dug into my wrist and I hit my head off the ceiling of the car. I tried to close my eyes and rest, to keep my mind off of the pain from the cuffs, but that proved impossible when my head kept smacking on the car roof.

My second option was to just watch out the window at the trees that passed by. It was a good thing that I paid attention now because everything very quickly felt wrong. We were not going in the direction of the station or prison. We were not even getting on the highway. We kept turning down different back roads, away from any other cars.

I took a closer look around the car and even at the two uniforms. The radio in the vehicle had been removed and replaced with some other weird device. Neither man's uniform actually bore the insignia of any local Department nor the State Department.

Great! I thought. *This shit again.*

Unperturbed, I leaned my head against the windowpane, trying not to show any evidence that I had picked up on anything. Watching the trees, I started to notice a black figure behind every other tree we passed, getting closer, like a rotoscope. It bore the same white dots in its deep, dark eyes. I looked back to the front of the car for a second, seeing if either of them had picked up on anything out of the ordinary, but neither of them said anything or showed any movement other than scratching their noses. I turned back to the forest to see this figure now right outside the window, as if hanging on through suction cupped fingers. I scurried to the other side of the car; it watched me with intensity.

The driver looked in the rearview mirror to see me moving as I did and then saw the thing hanging on to the side. I looked to him through the rearview. We were approaching a bend to an overhead bridge.

"The fu—" he started.

"Watch the road!" the other shouted, jerking the wheel, swerving around something.

Next I knew, we were tumbling over the road, rolling over and over. Since there was no roll cage, the car crumpled and crunched in on itself. Glass shattered, metal scraped on metal and asphalt until we smashed into the brick frame of an overhead bridge.

My neck was broken, along with a few ribs. My arms were, too, one dislocated. Glass stabbed through my eye. And some had slit up my arms and wrists; the force of the rolling had caused the skin around one of the cuffs to peel off like a glove, through the cuff, but held on at my fingertips. Bone, muscle, veins, and blood were left bare. The driver was screaming quietly as his life faded from the steering column jabbed through his chest and lungs. The other was unmoving, unconscious, breathing, but otherwise unscraped.

I lay there, feeling the blood leak from my hand and other orifices over my body. Blood flowing from my eye and nose. The driver stopped screaming, I presumed he passed, and the one in the passenger seat started to wake up. He looked around, dazed, and looked at me. Panic overtook him as I laughed, staring at him.

"Want to see a magic trick?" I asked him.

Before he could answer, I snapped my own neck back into position, and took the shard of glass from my eye. Blood spurted like an old, tense pimple being popped. I put my flesh-deprived hand over the damaged eye. I slowly lifted it to show a perfectly working eye. I crossed my eyes and pursed my lips like a fish, flopping my arms. The bones cracked and protested as they snapped back into the correct position and back in socket. The man watched in horror, becoming Catholic as he made the sign of the cross and shouted the Lord's Prayer.

I whistled. He looked at me. I gripped the torn flesh with teeth and yanked, blood whipping over the man's face and part of the car. The man threw up, while he was still on his side, but still kinda upside down. His puke ran down, or up, his face, some leaking into his nose. The flesh grew back around my hand, growing like vines until it formed flesh.

"Ta-dah!" I said, wiggling my fingers at him.

"Wh—what?" he asked.

And before I could ask, he was ripped from the vehicle. Watching him be taken by a large, seven-fingered hand, I was taken aback. I tried to open the door, but the car had collapsed enough to keep the doors stuck in place. I brought my legs to my chest and launched them straight out, crashing against the door, causing it to fly off into the air and come crashing down on the opposite side of the car. I then pulled myself out from the car, sitting on the frame as I swung my legs out over the side, and slid off onto the road, trying to keep my balance.

There was the sickening sound of crunching bone and flesh on flesh. The figure that I had been seeing, almost all in shadow, was now a shorter figure, resembling a woman. Hair about shoulder length. It was holding down the man it had yanked from the car, pounding into his face over and over with an open hand, like playing an arcade rhythm game, while choking him. The man was obviously already dead as each blow hit him like a meat tenderizer, making his face just more and more like a mush with pulverized bone marrow mixed in. This thing stopped and unhinged its mouth, picked up the man, and swallowed what was left of him like a snake. It was quick, too. One second the man was there, the next he was gone.

It turned slowly to me, its white-dotted eyes a full fiery red. It wasn't Raef; let alone not at all looking like him, he wouldn't be as brutish. I watched it as it rolled its neck. Going through everything in my mind, I couldn't connect it to anything. I took a shot in the dark.

"Sherman?"

It snapped its head at me, the dots now purple.

"Oh shit," I said as I started running, the asphalt quickly turning to a wood floor.

KORD

I followed Raef with caution, holding my lantern high and keeping some distance between us. I hummed to myself "Total Freedom" by Andrew W.K. to get my focus off of the sound of rubber soles on rock. The same sound I had been hearing for almost three days. I kept coughing up coal-covered mucus, and each time I did, I wanted to bash Raef's head in again.

At least now we were finally heading up. Every corridor we were taking was marked with a directional compass with an *M* accompanying it. We also kept coming to different crossroads in the caves that made me feel like I was playing a video game, but Raef just knew which way to go. I reached into my pocket and pulled out the flare gun, again; the cartridge was still in there.

Do not hold it against the man, a dull humming told me.

I didn't know what she meant, but I listened and kept following. Raef rubbed his upper arm and shoulder the entire time we moved. He stopped as we came to a not so high open room; it had five different corridors leading into it. I could hear rain.

"Kord," Raef said as he walked to a corridor opposite me.

I held out my lantern, which then illuminated most of the room, and I could see clearly what was around me and a little bit into each corridor. In the center of the room was a rectangular wooden box, rope tied around it, sitting on a perch of sticks and straw, and on the box was a large symbol that looked like a carpenter's compass. However, there were three obvious elements to it: a moon, a Star of David, and a Greek Cross. I began to approach the box.

"Kord! Don't!" A familiar voice said, but I couldn't tell who.

MARTIN

I finished hacking up my lungs from the tobacco stick and looked at the three of them: Clarkson, Theresa, and Smitt. Smitt rolled her eyes at me, and I knew that she wouldn't provide any help. Theresa and Clarkson looked to each other like they wanted to say something but couldn't spit it out.

"And believe me when I say I know you don't believe me, but soon enough you will," I said, taking another long drag of my cigarette.

There was silence from all the people in the room; it was instead filled with the pattering of rain against the windowpanes.

"Who were the three?" Theresa asked.

"Meyer. Your father, Sherman. And myself."

Someone was running down the halls, the floorboards creaking as they stepped.

"You really expect us to believe that—" Ms. Smitt was saying.

Meyer burst through the door, panting and slamming the door behind him. Everyone else stared at him with sheer confusion and immense surprise. I just looked at him. He was peering out through the door window and then ducking behind the door.

"Martin," he said.

"Meyer," I replied.

"We've got a problem. A big fucking problem."

"Let me guess. The consequences of Sherman?"

"Yeah, well, that's one. Damn thing is scary as shit."

"It's a cur—what do you mean one?"

"Kord's at the tomb."

"What tomb?" Clarkson asked.

"Raef's. Long story, tell you late—" Meyer was saying.

"I gave them the rundown, Meyer. How do you know he's there?"

"Look, Martin. Just…just trust me, okay?"

"You know something I don't."

"No shit, fuckwit."

Meyer grabbed my shirt, opened the door, and drug me out of the room and down the hall. The wooden floorboards turned to stone and everything became dark. We broke into a sprint toward a bright light. It was a lantern, and someone was holding it.

"Kord! Don't!" Meyer said as we ran into the room.

I saw Raef. My body went hot as I stomped my foot at him. Meyer moved between us, standing in front of another corridor.

KORD

Of all things I expected to see while I was down here, the Lieutenant Governor and some random man was not it. This other man seemed to have known Raef and vice versa. I stared at the two of them. At the moment, I didn't care. The pattering of rain gave me a hope I hadn't felt in a while. I wanted out. I would get out.

"Kord, don't touch that," Meyer said, holding out a hand.

"You might want to listen to the bastard," the other man said.

"Martin, some cooperation right now would be much appreciated."

Alright, so his name is Martin, I thought.

"Step on an egg, Meyer."

"Someone's touchy," Raef said.

"Fuck you," Meyer and Martin said in unison.

They stared each other down and I backed up from the box a bit. The rope on it had actually rotted away significantly. The wood was rotting as well, and there was an awful smell coming from it. There were more steps coming from the unblocked corridor. The three men all looked to it. Nothing emerged.

"I have some questions," I said. "Who are you?"

"We're ancient people from the ancient world, cursed to this earth. That's a quick gist of it," Martin said.

The footsteps kept coming.

"I'm just going to accept that, because," I said, sweeping my hand, then pointing to the box asking, "What's this?"

"My coffin," Raef said.

"Okay," I started, "so I'm going out on a limb here. Raef here is actually inside this casket, and you two are meant to not let him escape. I'm going to assume that me being in here is complicating things a lot more."

"Partially," Meyer said. "It's more my fault. I made a deal here with Raef—"

"I knew there was something—" Martin was saying.

"Shut up, Martin."

"No, you traitor. We're supp—"

"Let me—"

"No, you—"

"Both of you! Shut it!" I snapped.

They all looked at me.

"You, Meyer," I said, pointing at him, "You made a metaphorical deal with the devil. That's why I'm in here. And I'm going to unfortunately make it more complicated, aren't I?"

"No, actually. I messed up my end," Raef said with a very somber voice.

Martin and Meyer looked at him as if he were speaking pig Latin. The steps from the empty corridor stopped, and all three men looked down it as if Teddy Roosevelt had been resurrected—until I studied them closer. Each one had goose bumps, and each one seemed frozen in fear. I slowly turned, my lantern uncovering a woman about my height with shoulder-length hair. Its eyes were dark, black voids, with little white dots in them. Almost like the angel that had been looking over me. But it's face was just…static, like a TV static.

The thing was watching the three men, but when it turned to me, its white dots flashed pink, to blue, and then faded into normal, human, beautiful hazel eyes. The face melted into one I knew, its height stayed the same, and the hair turned from an oily, sleeky mess to a fluffy brown. It started to approach me.

"Abagail?" I asked it.

It nodded, still approaching me.

Martin, Meyer, and Raef were all terrified of this thing. Abagail Sherman was the eldest sister of the siblings. She had passed in 2021 in Oklahoma, officially from the pandemic, but there was no body for a coffin. The two of us had an odd relationship, but I never understood her relationship with Theresa and Clarkson. They never talked about it nor even talked to each other when I was around.

This thing, I thought posing as Abagail, came up to my side and wrapped me in a hug, crying. It wailed, softly hitting me. I hesitated at first, but wrapped my free arm around it, rubbing its back.

"Why is she here?" I asked to the three men.

"There were four of us, the fourth was—" Martin started.

"Her father. To put it in terms you'd understand: we are cursed. When we locked away Raef, we were made to always stay around to keep him concealed. If we were ever to have a family, we would die and leave a curse upon our first born."

Of course, it's the first born, I thought, but I didn't say anything. Abagail stopped crying, her warm hug grew cold, and she backed away from me to the corridor she had walked out from, reverting back to how she entered. All joy rushed from me when I saw the pain enter her eyes. I looked at the coffin in thought. I looked back to the men.

"You locked away fear. For decades, centuries, millennia. You locked away fear. Why?"

"Because, long story short, it's the Antichrist," Martin said.

I was about to say something but stopped. The coffin smelled of death, and whatever was inside, was obviously not alive. I thought for a second and finally asked, "Why shouldn't I touch it?"

"Because we can't let him out," Meyer said.

"But he's obviously been out. How is he trapped in here?" I asked.

Meyer and Martin both kept quiet, looking in opposite directions.

"What say you, Kord?" Raef asked.

I said nothing. I shined my light closer to a hole in the box and staring back at me was a skeleton. I stepped back from the coffin.

"I have an idea," I said.

I reached into my pocket, pulled out the flare gun, pointed it at the straw and sticks, and fired. All the other times, it didn't work, but this time, it went up in a roar of flames. The fire engulfed it and danced, singing to us. Abagail and I watched it with glee as it crackled and popped as if speaking to us. I pressed the release lever on the top of the flare gun and the barrel fell, the cartridge fell out when tipping it over, and it had actually fired.

I closed the barrel and held it for a bit. The room didn't fill with smoke. All of the smoke was floating up through a hole in the ceiling of the cave. The pattering of rain grew louder and louder, and my feet became wet. I scanned the room with the lantern, the three men were gone, and only Abagail was left. Through the staticky face, a smile had emerged. She approached me again, but she didn't change. Her eyes were dark voids with two blue dots that stared right at me. They were filled with immense sorrow, but part of them was also happy. As if happy to see me. She put a hand on the top of my head.

My head became light, my whole body became light. My vision blurred and came back to a light streaming onto my face. I was leaning on a rock, and my lantern was sitting on the ground next to me. Water had covered the floor of the cave, but not enough to move the lantern, just enough to seep into the top of my boots that laid almost flat on the ground. I looked around and found myself in a room that looked just like the one I was first trapped in. I got up and lifted the lantern around. Above the rocks in front of me was a carpenter's compass. I looked around. I sighed. I felt around on the rocks.

This one, Kord, a humming told me. There was a handprint over an etching of a carpenter's compass on one of the larger rocks at the top of the pile. I set my lantern down and put both hands on the larger rock. I pushed, and I pushed. It wouldn't budge.

I took in a deep breath, and just as something brushed my shirt, I threw all of my weight against the rock. It gave way, tumbling out into a pool of water, and I fell on top of it. Subsequent rocks fell in after it, making me a bridge of sorts through the mud. I stared flabbergasted out at the world, what little sunlight that was able to peer through the storm clouds in the distance stunned me.

I began to laugh, my stomach pressing hard into the rock. I rolled over, listening to the pattering rain in the creek, controlling my breathing. I grabbed my lantern and paused, seeing something out of the corner of my eye in the cave. The marionette lay on the floor, soaked, staring at me. I smiled and walked out of the cave, onto the rock, and into the rain. It stung at first, but it felt great feeling the dirt and coal dust run off me like paint.

I stood on the rocky shore that was being covered up with an ever-rising creek level, looking down at my kayak. It was still tied to a tree, and after shining the lantern in there to check for critters, and then lifting it just enough to drain the rainwater, I got inside it, put my bag in my lap, unclipped the oar from the side of the kayak, cut the line, and let myself float downstream. The rain still beat against my face, soaking me

THE TOMB · 217

and my pack. The kayak drifted naturally to the right side of the riverbank, floating under the canopy of trees and giving me shade from the rain.

I didn't keep track of time, I didn't care. Of all of the things that ran through my mind, Raef, Martin, Meyer, all of the burning, there was one thing that stuck out in my mind: "We'll Meet Again." I thought of my mom, and the rain provided the perfect cover for my eyes. I thought of Abagail, and I balled my fist from the confusion. I tried to think about being safe, about what lay ahead in the future. I was out. I was out! And yet, all I could think about was those I lost.

"I'm sorry," I muttered to myself.

I began to hear voices. I thought I went crazy until I found myself getting closer to a boat launch. They were strangers' voices.

"—and blue team, you'll be checking up the creek. Red team. You'll be searching—" a man was saying with others watching him.

I smiled, cutting him off when I jammed my oar into the muddy riverbank. They all looked at me. A gross, unkept looking young lad.

"What y'all doing?" I asked.

A paramedic stepped forward, holding a piece of paper. He looked from it to me over and over. I smiled.

"Am I under arrest?" I asked, chortling to myself.

"That's the boy! That's Kord!" the paramedic said.

"Hi."

The group tossed me a rope and pulled me up the boat launch. When I was up far enough, I stepped from the kayak. Others rushed to help me keep balanced and to an ambulance. As they checked me out, I felt dizzy, my head going lighter and lighter. They pulled my kayak up onto the grass and took out my pack, bringing it over to the ambulance.

"Oh, this must've fallen out," one woman said and brought over the flare gun I had been using.

I looked at it, to her, and took it. Examining the flare gun, I ignored all other sounds, voices, people, and things around me. I sighed, feeling conflicted about something I couldn't understand. I grabbed my pack, to the frustration of the paramedic who was trying to put an IV or something in my arm. The pack in my lap, I unzipped it, stuffing the flare gun inside. My mouth went dry, and I laughed. I laughed to myself, barely mustering a sound of my own. But internally, I was screaming. I was screaming as loud as I could.

After stuffing the flare gun in my pack, the head of the marionette wiggled in the corner. I wanted to destroy it. I wanted to burn it like everything else. And with every thought about it, my world blurred. The tunneling vision focusing on the marionette's head, everything else going dark, the little light left focusing in as two little white dots. I passed out to a raspy laughter in my ear.

CHAPTER 23

KORD RECOVERS

?

The walls were a sickly green, bleached from the constant exposure to eye-piercing, fluorescent lights that gave an insistent drone. The floor tiles were cold and shiny enough to act like a near-perfect mirror. The constant beeping and tapping of machines up and down the hallway would've been enough to drive anyone mad. Just like how being cooped up in the same damn place, in almost perfect dark, can drive you mad. For anyone at any age, it's not fun. And for anyone young, you can find yourself here when you're not careful.

A simple fun outing with friends into a cave, not meant to be entered by anyone, can lead to travesty. If you get past the snakes, the mammals, the fish, the debris, and the litter from those who don't care, consider yourself lucky. If you can trek through the mud that goes to your ankle without losing your shoe or even boot, you're blessed. And if you can get through the true innards of the cave entirely on your own, well you simply aren't alive, because you'd ask too much.

All except for one. He had very little help at all, and even then, others might not believe him.

"Hey, Kord. Kord! Wake up, man," Clarkson squeaked like a mouse.

He really does have a high-pitched voice now that I hear it for myself.

"Oy, Kord," Theresa said with a voice that could soothe angels.

A commotion came from his room at the end of the hall. It was short, but it was loud, and we didn't do anything about it since not many people were in that hall let alone on this floor. It was time for them to have their fun; they deserved it.

For as long as it had been, I couldn't just ruin their fun, now could I? But business is business, so I guess I had to crash the party.

Anytime someone walked down those halls, they made a thud on the tile. I make a clack. Anytime someone walked down that hallway, they walked slow. I walked at my pace. Anytime someone noticed the long shadows that are cast by decorations in the window, or occasional trashcan and chair, they think nothing more of them. I still have a special relationship with them. Oh, how it puts a smile on my face.

A smile that for the common man would come from seeing friends reunite. There's nothing special about the room. It's a one-occupant room, and there are two windows: one is at the end of the room and opens a few inches, and the other is behind and right above the bed and doesn't open at all. Clarkson's and Theresa's shadows were short against the ground and faint. Kord had two shadows. Kord's shadow was long. Kord's shadow was wide. Kord's shadow was dark. Kord's shadow was scared.

And though his shadow was scared, Kord himself was good at hiding it. He didn't say anything when I popped into the doorway. Theresa and Clarkson did the same when they saw me, both still having a smile across their faces.

"If you two wouldn't mind, I need to talk with the patient privately," I told them.

Theresa and Clarkson just nodded and left, telling Kord, "See ya in a bit."

I sat down in a chair next to Kord, waiting for the door to close. When the latch clicked a second time, it locked. Kord and I had an impromptu staring contest. No one said a word, and Kord, it seemed, didn't dare to. Till he did, of course.

"Now you're in my domain, Raef."

I couldn't help but chortle at that and said, "Is that so?"

"Yes."

"You are quite sure of yourself, aren't you? Well, I would be, too, if in your shoes."

I took out a normal, inconspicuous, empty syringe. I pulled it out from inside the wool garb I had on.

"You had me in the cave for a good while, but you couldn't keep up, and you know it," Kord said in an increasingly pompous voice.

"Mhm?"

"You can try to scare me or make me question what I know is fact all you want, Raef. It's not going to work on me now, now that I know who, well, *what* you actually are."

"Color me impressed, Kord. I'm listening," I said and crossed my legs, tapping the syringe against the bed frame.

"In that cave is darkness. You cannot see where you're going, and you get scared. That's your domain, darkness. You feed on that and present yourself as something safe, something tangible, something true. All the while you play mind games on them, making them think that there is no way out. Well, I found a way," he said and lunged forward, grabbing my garb by the collar and getting in my face. "I *found*. A way."

When he finished, a large grin grew across his face. Two buck teeth grabbed my attention away from his overly bushy eyebrows and eyes. Each pupil reflected the light just right to glisten like stars through a Bengalese summer night.

"Kord," I started, with him still in my face, "you did as I wanted. And you're right, you got out. What you gave me in the meantime was quite…delectable. And you are right, you entered my domain, but you directly entered this time."

He tried to throw me from his face, but just launched himself back and fell to the bed. He bounced once and settled uncomfortably in it.

"When I first saw you, Kord, I watched from the corn. You were young. You were damaged. You were sad, and you were scared," I said and readjusted my garb by shifting my shoulders, "I stayed with you for quite a while, as you discovered. I was your personal Black Knight Satellite. You just made things so easy. But one way or another, you were able to fight me, and you fought hard. Then came just a few days ago, and you and your friends were floating down the creek. Oh, how I longed again to feed so well on something. Getting people en masse is fine, sure, but when you can taste them individually, it's just so mouthwatering that you can't resist.

"And you came directly into my home, and that's where you are so wrong, my young friend. My home is not the darkness, though it certainly helps. No, no. My home lies where people are afraid in general. I live in the uncertainty and unknown. Few are brave enough to go through it alone, and it is by learning and being patient that you stood a chance against me. I thought I told you this?"

I looked down at him through faux glasses and flicked the syringe tip. He couldn't hide it no more.

"Oh, now you get it. I told you I'm an excellent liar. But I do have two sides, as you know. One that feeds on your ignorance and arrogance. The other is what makes you grow. Both are equally fun for me. Some think I'm entirely evil, and so they try to rid me by using the same means I thrive by. The two were smart in one thing, keep me in check. Sometimes they're more successful than others. But they failed ultimately, it seems. For though I tell you my home is really everywhere, they had me trapped for the longest time in that cave. I had my agents, but it wasn't my sole work. Alas, Kord, it was you all along. You were my passport to freedom."

I pulled the back of the syringe in the air, and it filled with a liquid.

"I just have to run one test, Kord. I'm sure you wouldn't mind. Right now, you do not know what's in here. I do."

I grabbed his wrist closest to me, and gently turned it over, revealing the underside of his forearm. I grabbed his other hand and positioned it around the syringe. Together we slid the needle seamlessly into his skin. His eyes were locked on mine, and mine on his.

"One of two things can happen now. Listen closely, Kord. Either you come back down the hallway with me, through the valley again, or you stay here, and Clarkson and Theresa can come back in. Do you understand?"

"Yes. But what will happen to you?"

"It will depend."

I put the slightest pressure onto his thumb, on the top of this scale of life. He was the one who pressed it the rest of the way. He did not flinch. He did not tense up.

I smiled. So, did he.

The syringe slid out, and his eyes drew heavy to close. I looked back to the wall, to his shadows. The second shadow smiled back.

"You were scared, Kord. You haven't learned, have you."

When I stood, the shadow was no longer a shadow. It stood there, shorter than usual, a face of static and dark voids of eyes with two white dots in them. The dots turned purple, and it nodded back toward Kord, who sighed deeply then spoke to me.

"You're not out of my life, but you're no longer in control. Because I know that I am never alone, fear."

ACKNOWLEDGMENTS

The process of writing *The Cave of Appalachia* has been a long and complex one. Many scenes have undergone multiple revisions—some only seen by my own eyes—and others have been completely scrapped. However, in the end, I have achieved something that very few people actually will, and I couldn't have done it without moral and financial support from several people.

Among the specifics, I would like to thank my family and friends as a whole for not letting me quit. I would also like to thank the Edinboro University of Pennsylvania for helping me meet a vast reach of new people—students, staff, and professors alike—that have helped me become who I am and achieve what I want.

I would also like to thank the following family, friends, colleagues, and new acquaintances who have supported me financially in getting the book itself published. Without them, you would never be able to have read this book. I don't know if they would like you walking up to them on the street and thanking them in person but give them a little thought in your mind.

In alphabetical order by last name, these great people are: Tony Biebel, Nall Bogart, Jacob Brucklacher, Nadine C

Buckley, Ian Bush, Taylor Carpenter, Keely Counter, Ryan A. Curry, Pamela Curry, Sean Curry, Timothy Feese, Hannah Flynn, Tara Hildebrand, Eric Koester, Dustin Norris, Andie Pawlyshn, Dylan Keith Ritenour, Michael Weger, and Julia Weller.